T0090165

By: Robert DuPrey, Ph.D.

BASIS FOR PROJECT MANAGEMENT AND APPLICATION DEVELOPMENT METHODOLOGY

- Project Integration Management
- Project Scope Management
- Project Time Management
- Project Cost Management
- Project Quality Management
- Project Human Resource Management
- Project Communications Management
- Project Risk Management
- Project Procurement Management
- Application Development Methodology

Basis for Project Management
And Application Development Methodology

Order this book online at www.trafford.com
or email orders@trafford.com

Most Trafford titles are also available at major online book retailers.

© Copyright 2010 Robert DuPrey.
Book design by Robert DuPrey
Cover design and illustration by Robert DuPrey
All rights reserved. No part of this publication may be reproduced, stored in a retrieval
system, or transmitted, in any form or by any means, electronic, mechanical, photocopying,
recording, or otherwise, without the written prior permission of the author.

Printed in the United States of America.

ISBN: 978-1-4269-3214-4 (sc)

ISBN: 978-1-4269-3215-1 (e-book)

*Our mission is to efficiently provide the world's finest, most comprehensive book publishing
service, enabling every author to experience success. To find out how to publish your book,
your way, and have it available worldwide, visit us online at www.trafford.com*

Trafford rev. 7/9/2010

 www.trafford.com

North America & international
toll-free: 1 888 232 4444 (USA & Canada)
phone: 250 383 6864 ♦ fax: 812 355 4082

I dedicate this book to those who are using this
book and wanting to be a great Project Manager

BASIS FOR PROJECT MANAGEMENT

PREFACE

This book "Basis for Project Management" is written to describe tasks and activities that are involved in managing a project. Project could be Information Technology (IT) or a non-IT, but the fundamentals and basis for project management should be the same. This book has diagrams with emphasis to terms such as "Activities", "Tools/Techniques" and "Results". Activities and Results are referred to as documents (e.g., a scope statement) or documentable items (e.g., activity dependencies). "Tools/Techniques" are the mechanisms applied to the activities to create the results. In addition to its fundamental simplicity, this approach offers several other benefits:

- It emphasizes the interactions among the process areas. Results from one process become activities to another process.
- The structure is flexible and robust. Changes in process and practice can be accommodated by adding a new process, by re-sequencing processes, by subdividing processes, or by adding descriptive tasks or activities within a process.
- Processes are at the core of other standards. For example, the International Organization for Standardization's quality standards (ISO series - 1994) are based on identification of business processes.

When it comes to Work Breakdown Structures, Network diagrams, and S-Curves, a picture is worth a thousand words.

Note:

Some of the project management specific information that was gathered in this book came from many sources. Refer to "Reference" section in order to locate the source of information. Author apologizes in advance for names and/or sources of information that he may have omitted in this book.

PROJECT MANAGEMENT CONCEPTS

NINE MAIN PROJECT MANAGEMENT AREAS

APPLICATION SOFTWRE DEVELOPMENT

An Overview of Basis for Project Management

Project Integration Management

A subset of project management that includes the processes required to ensure that the various elements of the project are properly coordinated. It consists of:

- Project Plan Development: Taking the results of other planning processes and putting them into a consistent, coherent document.
- Project Plan Execution: Carrying out the project plan by performing the activities included therein.
- Overall Change Control: Coordinating changes across the entire project.

Project Scope Management

A subset of project management that includes the processes required to ensure that the project includes all the work required, and to complete the project successfully. It consists of:

- Scope Planning: Developing a written scope statement as the basis for future project decisions.
- Scope Definition: Subdividing the major project deliverables into smaller, more manageable components.
- Scope Verification: Formalizing acceptance of the project scope.
- Scope Change Control: Controlling changes to project scope.

Project Time Management

A subset of project management that includes the processes required to ensure timely completion of the project. It consists of:

- Activity Definition: Identifying the specific activities that must be performed to produce the various project deliverables.
- Activity Sequencing: Identifying and documenting interactivity dependencies.
- Activity Duration Estimating: Estimating the number of work periods which will be needed to complete individual activities.
- Schedule Development: Analyzing activity sequences, activity durations, and resource requirements to create the project schedule.
- Schedule Control: Controlling changes to the project schedule.

Project Cost Management

A subset of project management that includes the processes required to ensure that the project is completed within the approved budget. It consists of:

- Resource Planning: Determining what resources (people, equipment, materials) and what quantities of each should be used to perform project activities.
- Cost Estimating: Developing an approximation (estimate) of the costs of the resources needed to complete project activities.
- Cost Budgeting: Allocating the overall cost estimate to individual work items.
- Cost Control: Controlling changes to the project budget.

Project Quality Management

A subset of project management that includes the processes required to ensure that the project will satisfy the needs for which it was undertaken. It consists of:

- Quality Planning: Identifying which quality standards are relevant to the project and determining how to satisfy them.
- Quality Assurance: Evaluating overall project performance on a regular basis to provide confidence that the project will satisfy the relevant quality standards.
- Quality Control: Monitoring specific project results to determine if they comply with relevant quality standards and identifying ways to eliminate causes of unsatisfactory performance.

Project Human Resource Management

A subset of project management that includes the processes required to make the most effective use of the people involved with the project. It consists of:

- Organizational Planning: Identifying, documenting, and assigning project roles, responsibilities, and reporting relationships.
- Staff Acquisition: Getting the human resources needed assigned to and working on the project.
- Team Development: Developing individual and group skills to enhance project performance.

Project Communications Management

A subset of project management that includes the processes required to ensure timely and appropriate generation, collection, dissemination, storage, and ultimate disposition of project information. It consists of:

- Communications Planning: Determining the information and communications needs of the stakeholders who need what information, when will they need it, and how will it be given to them.
- Information Distribution: Making needed information available to project stakeholders in a timely manner.
- Performance Reporting: Collecting and disseminating performance information. This includes status reporting, progress measurement, and forecasting.
- Administrative Closure: Generating, gathering, and disseminating information to formalize phase or project completion.

Project Risk Management

A subset of project management that includes the processes concerned with identifying, analyzing, and responding to project risk. It consists of:

- Risk Identification: Determining which risks are likely to affect the project and documenting the characteristics of each.
- Risk Quantification: Evaluating risks and risk interactions to assess the range of possible project outcomes.
- Risk Response Development: Defining enhancement steps for opportunities and responses to threats.
- Risk Response Control: Responding to changes in risk over the course of the project.

Project Procurement Management

A subset of project management that includes the processes required to acquire goods and services from outside the performing organization. It consists of:

- Procurement Planning: Determining what to procure and when.
- Solicitation Planning: Documenting product requirements and identifying potential sources.
- Solicitation: obtaining quotations, bids, offers, or proposals as appropriate.
- Source Selection: Choosing from among potential sellers.
- Contract Administration: Managing the relationship with the seller.
- Contract Close-out: Completion and settlement of the contract, including resolution of any open items.

Application Development Methodologies

- Waterfall: Linear framework type.
- Prototyping: Iterative framework type
- Incremental: Combination of linear and iterative framework type
- Spiral: Combination linear and iterative framework type
- Rapid Application Development (RAD): Iterative framework type

CHAPTER 1

INTRODUCTION

The *Basis for Project Management* is an inclusive term that describes the knowledge base for all tasks and activities needed within the profession of project management. As with other professions such as law, medicine, and accounting to Duncan (1996) "the body of knowledge rests with the practitioners and academics that apply and advance it". The Basis for project management includes knowledge of proven, traditional practices which are widely applied as well as knowledge of innovative and advanced practices which have seen more limited use.

This book is written on chapters. There are 13 chapters and are separated such that the reader can refer to each chapter for a specific topic and also for the ease of reading.

This chapter defines and explains several key terms and provides an overview of the rest of the book. It includes the following major sections:

- Purpose of this Book
- What is a Project?
- What is Project Management?
- Relationship to Other Management Disciplines
- Related Endeavors

PURPOSE OF THIS BOOK

The primary purpose of this book is to identify and describe all tasks and activities that are acceptable and needed to manage a project. The term acceptable means that the knowledge and practices described are applicable to most projects most of the time.

This book is also intended to provide a common lexicon within the profession for talking about project management. Project management is a relatively young profession, and while there is substantial commonality around what is done, there is relatively little commonality in the terms used.

This book provides a basic reference for anyone interested in the profession of project management. This includes, but is not limited to:

- Project managers and other project team members.
- Managers of project managers.
- Project customers and other project stakeholders.
- Functional managers with employees assigned to project teams.
- Educators teaching project management and related subjects.
- Consultants and other specialists in project management and related fields.
- Trainers developing project management educational programs.

As a basic reference, this book is neither comprehensive nor all-inclusive. Appendix A discusses application area extensions while list of sources of information in reference section will provide further information on project management.

This book will provide a consistent structure for professional development programs including:

- Certification of Project Management Professionals (PMPs).
- Accreditation of degree granting educational programs in project management.

WHAT IS A PROJECT?

Organizations Perform Work

Work generally involves either *operations* or *projects*, although the two may overlap. Operations and projects share many characteristics; for example, they are:

- Performed by people.
- Constrained by limited resources.
- Planned, executed, and controlled.

Operations and projects differ primarily in that operations are ongoing and repetitive while projects are temporary and unique. A project can thus be defined in terms of its distinctive characteristics. According to The American Heritage Dictionary of the English Language "a *project is a temporary endeavor undertaken to create a unique product or service. Temporary* means that every project has a definite beginning and a definite end". According to the same source *Unique* means that "the product or service is different in some distinguishing way from all similar products or services".

Projects are undertaken at all levels of the organization. They may involve a single person or many thousands. They may require less than 100 hours to complete or over 10,000,000 hours. Projects may involve a single unit of one organization or may cross organizational boundaries as in joint ventures and partnering. Projects are often critical components of the performing organization's business strategy. Examples of projects include:

- Developing a new product or service.
- Effecting a change in structure, staffing, or style of an organization.
- Designing a new transportation vehicle.
- Developing or acquiring a new or modified information system.
- Constructing a building or facility.
- Running a campaign for political office.
- Implementing a new business procedure or process.

Temporary

According to The American Heritage Dictionary of the English Language *Temporary* means that every project has "a definite beginning and a definite end". The end is reached when the project's objectives have been achieved, or when it becomes clear that the project objectives will not or cannot be met and the project is terminated.

Temporary does not necessarily mean short in duration; many projects last for several years. In every case, however, the duration of a project is finite; projects are not ongoing efforts.

In addition, temporary does not generally apply to the product or service created by the project. Most projects are undertaken to create a lasting result. For example, a project to erect a national monument will create a result expected to last centuries. Many undertakings are temporary in the sense that they will end at some point. For example, assembly work at an automotive plant will eventually be discontinued, and the plant itself decommissioned. Projects are fundamentally different because the project ceases when its declared objectives have been attained, while non-project undertakings adopt a new set of objectives and continue to work.

The temporary nature of projects may apply to other aspects of the endeavor as well:

- The opportunity or market window is usually temporary - most projects have a limited time frame in which to produce their product or service.
- The project team, as a team, seldom outlives the project - most projects are performed by a team created for the sole purpose of performing the project, and the team is disbanded and members reassigned when the project is complete.

Unique Product or Service

Projects involve doing something which has not been done before and which is, therefore, unique. A product or service may be unique even if the category it belongs to is large. For example, many thousands of office buildings have been developed, but each individual facility is unique - different owner, different design, different location, different contractors, and so on. The presence of repetitive elements does not change the fundamental uniqueness of the overall effort. For example:

- A project to develop a new commercial airliner may require multiple prototypes.
- A project to bring a new drug to market may require thousands of doses of the drug to support clinical trials.
- A real estate development project may include hundreds of individual units.

Because the product of each project is unique, the characteristics that distinguish the product or service must be progressively elaborated. According to American Heritage Dictionary of the English Language (1992) Progressively means "proceeding in steps; continuing steadily by increments" while elaborated means "worked out with care and detail; developed thoroughly". These distinguishing characteristics will be broadly defined early in the project and will be made more explicit and detailed as the project team develops a better and more complete understanding of the product.

Progressive elaboration of product characteristics must be carefully coordinated with proper project scope definition, particularly if the project is performed under contract. When properly defined, the scope of the project - the work to be done should remain constant even as the product characteristics are progressively elaborated.

The relationship between product scope and project scope is discussed further in the introduction to Chapter 5.

The following two examples illustrate progressive elaboration in two different application areas.

Example 1

A chemical processing plant begins with process engineering to define the characteristics of the process. These characteristics are used to design the major processing units. This information becomes the basis for engineering design which defines both the detail plant layout and the mechanical characteristics of the process units and ancillary facilities. All of these result in design drawings which are elaborated to produce fabrication drawings (construction isometrics). During construction, interpretations and adaptations are made as needed and subject to proper approval. This further elaboration of the characteristics is captured by "as built" drawings. During test and turnover, further elaboration of the characteristics is often made in the form of final operating adjustments.

Example 2

The product of a biopharmaceutical research project may initially be defined as "clinical trials of xyz" since the number of trials and the size of each is not known. As the project proceeds, the product may be described more explicitly as "three Phase-I trials, four Phase-II trials, and two Phase-III trials." The next round of progressive elaboration might focus exclusively on the protocol for the Phase-I trials - how many patients get what dosages and how frequently. In the project's final stages, the Phase-III trials would be explicitly defined based on information gathered and analyzed during the Phase-I and Phase-II trials.

WHAT IS PROJECT MANAGEMENT?

Project management is the application of knowledge, skills, tools, and techniques to project activities in order to meet or exceed stakeholder needs and expectations from a project. Meeting or exceeding stakeholder needs and expectations invariably involves balancing competing demands among:

- Scope, time, cost, and quality.
- Stakeholders with differing needs and expectations.
- Identified requirements (needs) and unidentified requirements (expectations).

The term *project management* is sometimes used to describe an organizational approach to the management of ongoing operations. This approach, more properly called *management by projects,* treats many aspects of ongoing operations as projects in order to apply project management to them. Although an understanding of project management is obviously critical to an organization that is managing by projects, a detailed discussion of the approach itself is outside the scope of this book.

Knowledge about project management can be organized in many ways. This book has 3 initial chapters known as project management framework sections and 8 major project management chapters and chapter 13 that discusses application development methodologies.

The Project Management Framework

The Project Management Framework provides a basic structure for understanding project management.

Chapter 1, Introduction, defines key terms and provides an overview of the rest of the book.

Chapter 2, The Project Management Context, describes the environment in which projects operate. The project management team must understand this broader context-managing the day-to-day activities of the project is necessary for success but not sufficient.

Chapter 3, Project Management Processes, describes a generalized view of how the various project management processes commonly interact. Understanding these interactions is essential to understanding the material presented in Chapters 4 through 12. Chapter 13 is specific to Information Systems Development Methodologies.

Project Management Process Areas

This book "Basis for Project Management" describes project management processes areas and practice in terms of its component within the processes. These processes have been organized into nine project management based areas with three initial sections as introduction sections as described in chapters below and as illustrated in Figure 1-1.

Chapter 4, Project Integration Management, describes the processes required to ensure that the various elements of the project are properly coordinated. It consists of project plan development, project plan execution, and overall change control.

Chapter 5, Project Scope Management, describes the processes required to ensure that the project includes all the work required, and only the work required, to complete the project successfully. It consists of initiation, scope planning, scope definition, scope verification, and scope change control.

Chapter 6, Project Time Management, describes the processes required to ensure timely completion of the project. It consists of activity definition, activity sequencing, activity duration estimating, schedule development, and schedule control.

Chapter 7, Project Cost Management, describes the processes required to ensure that the project is completed within the approved budget. It consists of resource planning, cost estimating, cost budgeting, and cost control.

Chapter 8, Project Quality Management, describes the processes required to ensure that the project will satisfy the needs for which it was undertaken. It consists of quality planning, quality assurance, and quality control.

Figure 1-1: Overview of Project Management Knowledge Areas and Project Management Processes

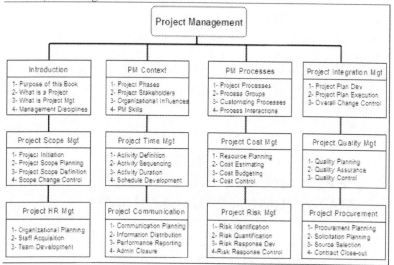

Chapter 9, Project Human Resource Management, describes the processes required to make the most effective use of the people involved with the project. It consists of organizational planning, staff acquisition, and team development.

Chapter 10, Project Communications Management, describes the processes required to ensure timely and appropriate generation, collection, dissemination, storage, and ultimate disposition of project information. It consists of communications planning, information distribution, performance reporting, and administrative closure.

Chapter 11, Project Risk Management, describes the processes concerned with identifying, analyzing, and responding to project risk. It consists of risk identification, risk quantification, risk response development, and risk response control.

Chapter 12, Project Procurement Management, describes the processes required to acquire goods and services from outside the performing organization. It consists of procurement planning, solicitation planning, solicitation, source selection, contract administration, and contract close-out.

PROJECT MANAGEMENT RELATIONSHIP TO OTHER MANAGEMENT DISCIPLINES

Much of the knowledge needed to manage projects is unique or nearly unique to project management (e.g., critical path analysis and work breakdown structures). However, the project management does overlap other management disciplines as illustrated in Figure 1-2.

General management encompasses planning, organizing, staffing, executing, and controlling the operations of an ongoing enterprise. General management also includes supporting disciplines such as computer programming, law, statistics and probability theory, logistics, and personnel. The project management overlaps general management in many areas-organizational behavior, financial forecasting, and planning techniques to name just a few. Chapter 2 provides a more detailed discussion of general management.

Application areas are categories of projects that have common elements significant in such projects but not needed or present in all projects. Application areas are usually defined in terms of:

- Technical elements, such as software development, pharmaceuticals, or construction engineering.
- Management elements, such as government contracting or new product development.
- Industry groups, such as automotive, chemicals, or financial services.

Related Endeavors

Certain types of endeavors are closely related to projects. These related undertakings are described below.

Programs

According to Turner (1992) "A *program* is a group of projects managed in a coordinated way to obtain benefits not available from managing them individually". Many programs also include elements of ongoing operations. For example:

- The "xyz airplane program" includes both the project and projects to design and develop the aircraft as well as the ongoing manufacturing and support of that craft in the field.
- Many electronics firms have "program managers" who are responsible for both individual product releases (projects) and the coordination of multiple releases over time (an ongoing operation).

Figure 1-2. Relationship of Project Management to Other
Management Disciplines

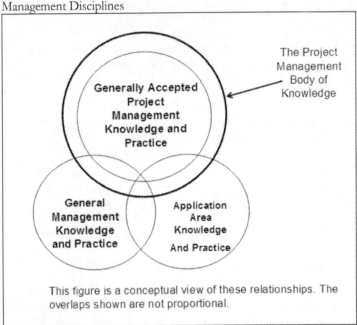

This figure is a conceptual view of these relationships. The overlaps shown are not proportional.

This figure is a conceptual *view* of these relationships. The overlaps shown are not proportional. Programs may also involve a series of repetitive or cyclical undertakings, for example:

- Utilities often speak of an annual "construction program," a regular, ongoing operation which involves many projects.
- Many non-profit organizations have a "fundraising program," an ongoing effort to obtain financial support that often involves a series of discrete projects such as a membership drive or an auction.
- Publishing a newspaper or magazine is also a program - the periodical itself is an ongoing effort, but each individual issue is a project. In some

application areas, program management and project management are treated as synonyms; in others, project management is a subset of program management.

Occasionally, program management is considered a subset of project management. This diversity of meaning makes it imperative that any discussion of program management versus project management be preceded by agreement on a clear and consistent definition of each term.

Sub-Projects
Projects are frequently divided into more manageable components or *subprojects*. Subprojects are often contracted out to an external enterprise or to another functional unit in the performing organization. Examples of subprojects include:

- A single project phase (project phases are described in Chapter 2).
- The installation of plumbing or electrical fixtures on a construction project.
- Automated testing of computer programs on a software development project.
- High-volume pharmaceutical manufacturing to support clinical trials of a new drug during a research and development project. However, from the perspective of the performing organization, a subproject is often thought of more as a service than as a product, and the service is unique. Thus Subprojects are typically referred to as projects and managed as such.

CHAPTER 2

THE PROJECT MANAGEMENT CONTEXT

Projects and project management operate in an environment broader than that of the project itself. The project management team must understand this broader context - managing the day-to-day activities of the project is necessary for success but not sufficient. This chapter describes key aspects of the project management context not covered elsewhere in this book. The topics included here are:

- Project Phases and the Project Life Cycle
- Project Stakeholders
- Organizational Influences
- Key General Management Skills
- Socioeconomic Influences

PROJECT PHASES AND THE PROJECT LIFE CYCLE

Because projects are unique undertakings, they involve a degree of uncertainty. Organizations performing projects will usually divide each project into several *project phases* to provide better management control and appropriate links to the ongoing operations of the performing organization. Collectively, the project phases are known as the *project life cycle*.

Characteristics of Project Phases

Each project phase is marked by completion of one or more *deliverables*. A deliverable is a tangible, verifiable work product such as a feasibility study, a detail design, or a working prototype. The deliverables, and hence the phases, are part of a generally sequential logic designed to ensure proper definition of the product of the project.

The conclusion of a project phase is generally marked by a review of both key deliverables and project performance in order to (a) determine if the project should continue into its next phase and (b) detect and correct errors cost effectively. These phase-end reviews are often called *phase exits, stage gates,* or *kill points.*

Each project phase normally includes a set of defined work products designed to establish the desired level of management control. The majority of these items are related to the primary phase deliverable, and the phases typically take their names from these items: requirements, design, build text, start-up, turnover, and others as appropriate. Several representative project life cycles are described in Chapter 2.

Characteristics of the Project Life Cycle

The project life cycle serves to define the beginning and the end of a project. For example, when an organization identifies an opportunity that it would like to respond to, it will often authorize a feasibility study to decide if it should undertake a project. The project life cycle definition will determine whether the feasibility study is treated as the first project phase or as a separate, stand-alone project.

The project life cycle definition will also determine which transitional actions at the end of the project are included and which are not. In this manner, the project life cycle definition can be used to link the project to the ongoing operations of the performing organization.

The phase sequence defined by most project life cycles generally involves some form of technology transfer or hand-off such as requirements to design, construction to operations, or design to manufacturing. Deliverables from the preceding phase are usually approved before work starts on the next phase. However, a subsequent phase is sometimes begun prior to approval of the previous phase deliverables when the risks involved are deemed acceptable. This practice of overlapping phases is often called *fast tracking.*

Project life cycles generally define:

- What technical work should be done in each phase (e.g., is the work of the architect part of the definition phase or part of the execution phase?).
- Who should be involved in each phase (e.g., concurrent engineering requires that the implementers be involved with requirements and design).

Project life cycle descriptions may be very general or very detailed. Highly detailed descriptions may have numerous forms, charts, and checklists to provide structure and consistency. Such detailed approaches are often called project management methodologies.
Most project life cycle descriptions share a number of common characteristics:

- Cost and staffing levels are low at the start, higher towards the end, and drop rapidly as the project draws to a conclusion. This pattern is illustrated in Figure 2-1.

Figure 2-1. Sample Generic Life Cycle

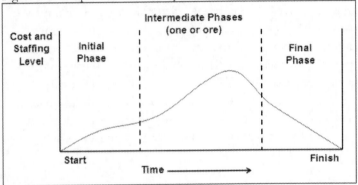

- The probability of successfully completing the project is lowest, and hence risk and uncertainty are highest, at the start of the project. The probability of successful completion generally gets progressively higher as the project continues.
- The ability of the stakeholders to influence the final characteristics of the project product and the final cost of the project is highest at the start and gets progressively lower as the project continues. A major contributor to this phenomenon is that the cost of changes and error correction generally increases as the project continues.

Care should be taken to distinguish the *project* life cycle from the *product* life cycle. For example, a project undertaken to bring a new desktop computer to market is but one phase or stage of the product life cycle.

Although many project life cycles have similar phase names with similar work products required, few are identical. Most have four or five phases, but some have nine or more. Even within a single application area there can be significant variations one organization's software development life cycle may have a single design phase while another's has separate phases for functional and detail design.

Subprojects within projects may also have distinct project life cycles. For example, an architectural firm hired to design a new office building is first involved in the owner's definition phase when doing the design and in the owner's implementation phase when supporting the construction effort. The architect's design project, however, will have its own series of phases from conceptual development through definition and implementation to closure. The architect may even treat designing the facility and supporting the construction as separate projects with their own distinct phases.

Representative Project Life Cycles

The following project life cycles have been chosen to illustrate the diversity of approaches in use. The examples shown are typical; they are neither recommended nor preferred. In each case, the phase names and major deliverables are those described by the author.

The U.S. Department of Defense describes a series of acquisition milestones and phases as illustrated in Figure 2-2.

Figure 2-2. Representative Life Cycle for Defense Acquisition, per US DOD

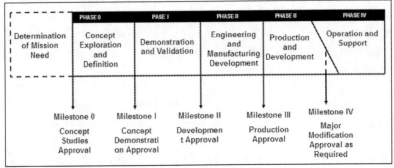

- Determination of Mission need - ends with Concept Studies Approval.
- Concept Exploration and Definition - ends with Concept Demonstration Approval.
- Demonstration and Validation - ends with Development Approval.
- Engineering and Manufacturing Development - ends with Production Approval.
- Production and Deployment - overlaps ongoing Operations and Support.

Morris (1981) describes a construction project life cycle in four stages as illustrated in Figure 2-3:

Figure 2-3. Representative Construction Project Life Cycle, per Morris

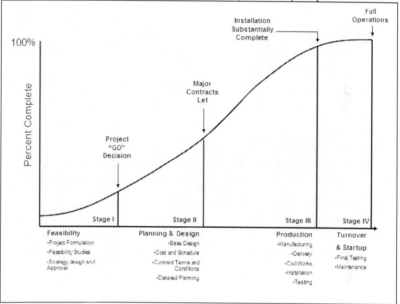

1. Feasibility - project formulation, feasibility studies, and strategy design and approval. A go/no-go decision is made at the end of this phase.
2. Planning and Design - base design, cost and schedule, contract terms and conditions, and detailed planning. Major contracts are let at the end of this phase.
3. Production - manufacturing, delivery, civil works, installation, and testing. The facility is substantially complete at the end of this phase.
4. Turnover and Start-up final testing and maintenance. The facility is in full operation at the end of this phase.

Murphy (1989) describes a project life cycle for pharmaceutical new product development in the United States as illustrated in Figure 2-4:

- Discovery and Screening - includes basic and applied research to identify candidates for preclinical testing.
- Preclinical Development - includes laboratory and animal testing to determine safety and efficacy as well as preparation and filing of an Investigational New Drug (IND) application.
- Registration(s) Workup - includes Clinical Phase-I, II, and III tests as well as preparation and filing of a New Drug Application (NDA).
- Post-submission Activity - includes additional work as required to support Food and Drug Administration (FDA) review of the NDA.

Figure 2-4. Representative Life Cycle for a Pharmaceuticals Project, per Murphy

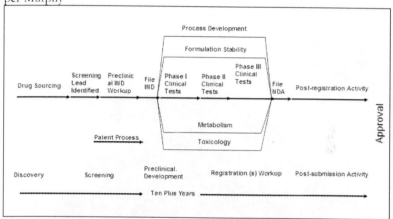

Software Application Development

Muench (1994) describes a spiral model (see Application Development Chapter 13) for software development with four cycles and four quadrants as illustrated in Figure 2-5:

Figure 2-5. Software Development Life Cycle

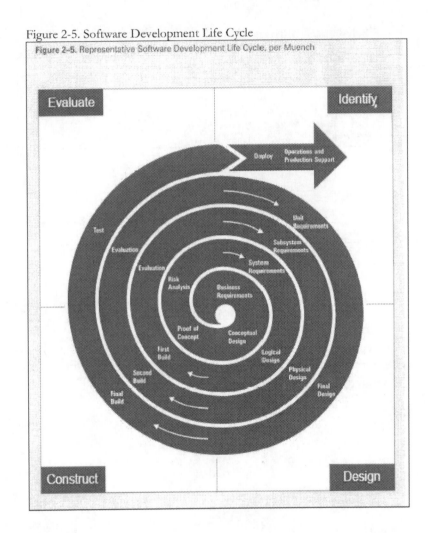

Figure 2-5. Representative Software Development Life Cycle, per Muench

1. Proof-of-concept cycle - capture business requirements, define goals for proof-of-concept, produce conceptual system design, design and construct the proof-of-concept, produce acceptance test plans, conduct risk analysis and make recommendations.

2. First build cycle - derive system requirements, define goals for first build, produce logical system design, design and construct the first build, produce system test plans, evaluate the first build and make recommendations.
3. Second build cycle - derive subsystem requirements, define goals for second build, produce physical design, construct the second build, produce system test plans, evaluate the second build and make recommendations.
4. Final cycle - complete unit requirements, final design, construct final build; perform unit, subsystem, system, and acceptance tests.

PROJECT STAKEHOLDERS

Project stakeholders are individuals and organizations who are actively involved in the project, or whose interests may be positively or negatively affected as a result of project execution or successful project completion. The project management team must identify the stakeholders, determine what their needs and expectations are, and then manage and influence those expectations to ensure a successful project.

Stakeholder identification is often especially difficult. For example, is an assembly line worker whose future employment depends on the outcome of a new product design project a stakeholder?

Key stakeholders on every project include:

- Project manager - the individual responsible for managing the project.

- Customer - the individual or organization that will use the project product. There may be multiple layers of customers. For example, the customers for a new pharmaceutical product may include the doctors who prescribe it, the patients who take it and the insurers who pay for it.
- Performing organization - the enterprise whose employees are most directly involved in doing the work of the project.
- Sponsor - the individual or group within the performing organization

In addition to these there are many different names and categories of project stakeholders - internal and external, owners and funders, suppliers and contractors, team members and their families, government agencies and media outlets, individual citizens, temporary or permanent lobbying organizations, and society at large.

The naming or grouping of stakeholders is primarily an aid to identifying which individuals and organizations view themselves as stakeholders. Stakeholder roles and responsibilities may overlap, as when an engineering firm provides financing for a plant it is designing. Managing stakeholder expectations may be difficult because stakeholders often have very different objectives that may come into conflict. For example:

- The manager of a department that has requested a new management information system may desire low cost, the system architect may emphasize technical excellence, and the programming contractor may be most interested in maximizing its profit.

- The vice president of research at an electronics firm may define new product success as state-of-the-art technology, the vice president of manufacturing may define it as world-class practices, and the vice president of marketing may be primarily concerned with the number of new features.

- The owner of a real estate development project may be focused on timely performance, the local governing body may desire to maximize tax revenue, an environmental group may wish to minimize adverse environmental impacts, and nearby residents may hope to relocate the project.

In general, differences between or among stakeholders should be resolved in favor of the customer. This does not, however, mean that the needs and expectations of other stakeholders can or should be disregarded. Finding appropriate resolutions to such differences can be one of the major challenges of project management.

ORGANIZATIONAL INFLUENCES

Projects are typically part of an organization larger than the project - corporations, government agencies, health care institutions, international bodies, professional associations, and others. Even when the project is the organization (joint ventures, partnering), the project will still be influenced by the organization or organizations that set it up. The following sections describe key aspects of these larger organizational structures that are likely to influence the project.

Organizational Systems

Project-based organizations are those whose operations consist primarily of projects.

These organizations fall into two categories:

1. Organizations that derive their revenue primarily from performing projects for others-architectural firms, engineering firms, consultants, construction contractors, government contractors, etc.
2. Organizations that have adopted *management by projects* (see Chapter 1). These organizations tend to have management systems in place to facilitate project management. For example, their financial systems are often specifically designed for accounting, tracking, and reporting on multiple simultaneous projects.

Non-project-based organizations - manufacturing companies, financial service firms, etc. seldom have management systems designed to support project needs efficiently and effectively. The absence of project-oriented systems usually makes project management more difficult. In some cases, non-project-based organizations will have departments or other sub-units that operate as project-based organizations with systems to match.

The project management team should be acutely aware of how the organization's systems affect the project. For example, if the organization rewards its functional managers for charging staff time to projects, the project management team may need to implement controls to ensure that assigned staffs are being used effectively on the project.

Organizational Cultures and Style

Most organizations have developed unique and describable cultures. These cultures are reflected in their shared values, norms, beliefs, and expectations; in their policies and procedures; in their view of authority relationships; and in numerous other factors.

Organizational cultures often have a direct influence on the project. For example:

- A team proposing an unusual or high-risk approach is more likely to secure approval in an aggressive or entrepreneurial organization.
- A project manager with a highly participative style is apt to encounter problems in a rigidly hierarchical organization, while a project manager with an authoritarian style will be equally challenged in a participative organization.

Organizational Structure

The structure of the performing organization often constrains the availability of or terms under which resources become available to the project. Organizational structures can be characterized as spanning a spectrum from *functional* to *project-based,* with a variety of matrix structures in between.

Figure 2-6 details key project-related characteristics of the major types of enterprise organizational structures. Project organization is discussed in Chapter 9, Organizational Planning.

Figure 2-6. Organizational Structure Influences on Projects

Organization Type / Project Charateristics	Functional	Matrix			Project-based
		Weak Matrix	Balanced Matrix	Stong Matrix	
Project Manager's Authority	Little or None	Limited	Low to Moderate	Moderate to High	High to Almost Total
Percent of Performing Organization's Personnel Assigned Full-time to Project Work	Virtually None	0-25%	15-60%	50-95%	85-100%
Project Manager's Role	Part-time	Part-time	Full-time	Full-time	Full-time
Common Titles for Project Manager's Role	Project Coordinator/ Project Leader	Project Coordinator/ Project Leader	Project Manager/ Project Officer	Project Manager/ Project Manager	Project Manager/ Project Manager
Project Management Administration Staff	Part-time	Part-time	Part-time	Part-time	Part-time

The classic *functional organization* shown in Figure 2-7 is a hierarchy where each employee has one clear superior. Staff is grouped by specialty, such as production, marketing, engineering, and accounting at the top level, with engineering further subdivided into mechanical and electrical. Functional organizations still have projects, but the perceived scope of the project is limited to the boundaries of the function: the engineering department in a functional organization will do its work independent of the manufacturing or marketing departments.

Figure 2-7. Functional Organization

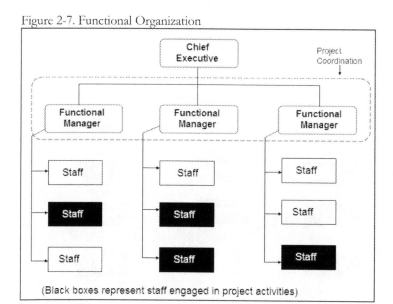

For example, when a new product development is undertaken in a purely functional organization, the design phase is often called a "design project" and includes only engineering department staff. If questions about manufacturing arise, they are passed up the hierarchy to the department head who consults with the head of the manufacturing department. The engineering department head then passes the answer back down the hierarchy to the engineering project manager.

At the opposite end of the spectrum is the *project-based organization* shown in Figure2-8.

Figure 2-8. Project-based Organization

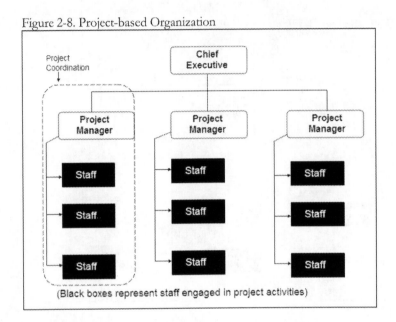

(Black boxes represent staff engaged in project activities)

In a *project-based* organization, team members are often collocated. Most of the organization's resources are involved in project work, and project managers have a great deal of independence and authority. *project-based* organizations often have organizational units called departments, but these groups either report directly to the project manager or provide support services to the various projects.

Matrix organizations as shown in Figures 2-9 through Figures 2-11 are a blend of functional and *project-based* characteristics. Weak matrices maintain many of the characteristics of a functional organization and the project manager role is more that of a coordinator or expediter than that of a manager. In similar fashion, strong matrices have many of the characteristics of the *project-based* organization-full-time project managers with considerable authority and full-time project administrative staff.

Figure 2-9. Weak Matrix Organization

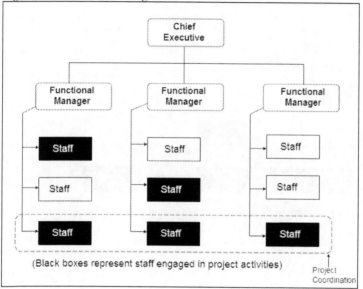

(Black boxes represent staff engaged in project activities)

Figure 2-10. Balanced Matrix Organization

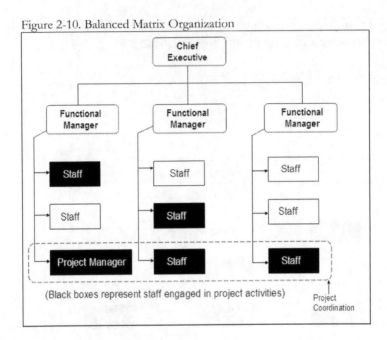

Figure 2-11. Strong Matrix Organization

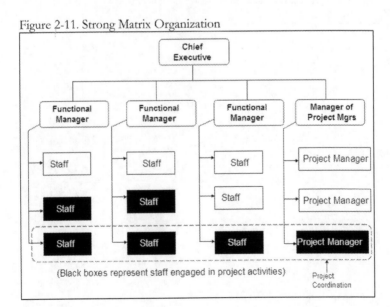

Most modern organizations involve all these structures at various levels as shown in Figure 2-12.

Figure 2-12. Composite Organization

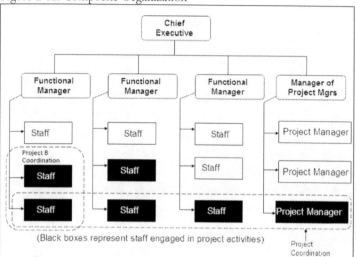

(Black boxes represent staff engaged in project activities)

For example, even a fundamentally functional organization may create a special project team to handle a critical project. Such a team may have many of the characteristics of a project in a *project-based* organization: it may include full-time staff from different functional departments; it may develop its own set of operating procedures, and it may operate outside the standard, formalized reporting structure.

KEY GENERAL MANAGEMENT SKILLS

General management is a broad subject dealing with every aspect of managing an ongoing enterprise. Among other topics, it includes:

- Finance and accounting, sales and marketing, research and development, manufacturing and distribution.
- Strategic planning, tactical planning, and operational planning.
- Organizational structures, organizational behavior, personnel administration, compensation, benefits, and career paths.
- Managing work relationships through motivation, delegation, supervision, team building, conflict management, and other techniques.
- Managing oneself through personal time management, stress management, and other techniques.

General management skills provide much of the foundation for building project management skills. They are often essential for the project manager. On any given project, skill in any number of general management areas may be required. This chapter describes key general management skills that are *highly likely to affect most projects* and that are not covered elsewhere. These skills are well documented in the general management literature and their application is fundamentally the same on a project.

There are also many general management skills that are relevant only on certain projects or in certain application areas. For example, team member safety is critical on virtually all construction projects and of little concern on most software development projects.

Leading

Kotter (1990) distinguishes between *leading* and *managing* while emphasizing the need for both: one without the other is likely to produce poor results. He says that managing s primarily concerned with "consistently producing key results expected by stakeholders," while leading involves:

- Establishing direction - developing both a vision of the future and strategies or producing the changes needed to achieve that vision.

- Aligning people - communicating the vision by words and deeds to all those cooperation may be needed to achieve the vision.

- Motivating and inspiring - helping people energize themselves to overcome political, bureaucratic, and resource barriers to change.

On a project, particularly a larger project, the project manager is generally expected to be the project's leader as well. Leadership is not, however, limited to the project manager: it may be demonstrated by many different individuals at many different times during the project. Leadership must be demonstrated at all levels of the project (project leadership, technical leadership, team leadership).

Communicating

Communicating involves the exchange of information. The sender is responsible for making the information clear, unambiguous, and complete so that the receiver can receive it correctly. The receiver is responsible for making sure that the information is received in its entirety and

understood   correctly.   Communicating   has   many
dimensions:

- Written and oral, listening and speaking.
- Internal (within the project) and external (to the customer, the media, the public, etc.).
- Formal (reports, briefings, etc.) and informal (memos, ad hoc conversations, etc.).
- Vertical (up and down the organization) and horizontal (with peers).

The general management skill of communicating is related to, but not the same as, Project Communications Management (described in Chapter 10). Communicating is the broader subject and involves a substantial body of knowledge that is not unique to the project context, for example:

- Sender-receiver models - feedback loops, barriers to communications, etc.
- Choice of media - when to communicate in writing, when to communicate orally, when to write an informal memo, when to write a formal report, etc.
- Writing style - active vs. passive voice, sentence structure, word choice, etc.
- Presentation techniques - body language, design of visual aids, etc.
- Meeting management techniques - preparing an agenda, dealing with conflict, etc.

Project   Communications   Management   is   the
application of these broad concepts to the specific needs

of a project; for example, deciding how, when, in what form, and to whom to report project performance.

Negotiating

Negotiating involves conferring with others in order to come to terms or reach an agreement.

Agreements may be negotiated directly or with assistance; mediation and arbitration are two types of assisted negotiation. Negotiations occur around many issues, at many times, and at many levels of the project. During the course of a typical project, project staffs are likely to negotiate for any or all of the following:

- Scope, cost, and schedule objectives.
- Changes to scope, cost, or schedule.
- Contract terms and conditions.
- Assignments.
- Resources.

Problem Solving

Problem solving involves a combination of problem definition and decision making. It is concerned with problems that have already occurred (as opposed to risk management that addresses potential problems).

Problem definition requires distinguishing between causes and symptoms. Problems may be internal (a key employee is reassigned to another project) or external (a permit required to begin work is delayed). Problems may be technical (differences of opinion about the best way to design a product), managerial (a functional group is not producing according to plan), or interpersonal (personality or style clashes).

Decision making includes analyzing the problem to identify viable solutions, and then making a choice from among them. Decisions can be made or obtained (from the customer, from the team, or from a functional manager). Once made, decisions must be implemented. Decisions also have a time element to them-the "right" decision may not be the "best" decision if it is made too early or too late.

Influencing the Organization

Influencing the organization involves the ability to "get things done." It requires an understanding of both the formal and informal structures of all the organizations involved - the performing organization, the customer, contractors, and numerous others as appropriate. Influencing the organization also requires an understanding of the mechanics of power and politics.

Both power and politics are used here in their positive senses. Pfeffer (1992) defines power as "the potential ability to influence behavior, to change the course of events, to overcome resistance, and to get people to do things that they would not otherwise do." In similar fashion, Eccles (1992) explains that "politics is about getting collective action from a group of people who may have quite different interests. It is about being willing to use conflict and disorder creatively. The negative sense, of course, derives from the fact that attempts to reconcile these interests result in power struggles and organizational games that can sometimes take on a thoroughly unproductive life of their own."

SOCIOECONOMIC INFLUENCES

Like general management, *socioeconomic influences* include a wide range of topics and issues. The project management team must understand that current conditions and trends in this area may have a major effect on their project; a small change can translate, usually with a time lag, into cataclysmic upheavals in the project itself.

Of the many potential socioeconomic influences, several major categories that frequently affect projects are described briefly below.

Standards and Regulations

Based on the International Organization for Standardization (1994) the difference between standards and regulations are as follow:

- A *standard* is a "document approved by a recognized body that provides, for common and repeated use, rules, guidelines, or characteristics for products, processes or services with which compliance is not mandatory." There are numerous standards in use covering everything from thermal stability of hydraulic fluids to the size of computer diskettes.

- A *regulation* is a "document which lays down product, process or service characteristics, including the applicable administrative provisions, with which compliance is mandatory." Building codes are an example of regulations.

- Care must be used in discussing standards and regulations since there is a vast gray area between the two, for example:

- Standards often begin as guidelines that describe a preferred approach, and later, with widespread adoption, become *de facto* regulations (e.g., the use of the Critical Path Method for scheduling major construction projects).
- Compliance may be mandated at different levels (e.g., by a government agency, by the management of the performing organization, or by the project management team).

For many projects, standards and regulations (by whatever definition) are well known and project plans can reflect their effects. In other cases, the influence is unknown or uncertain and must be considered under Project Risk Management.

Internationalization

As more and more organizations engage in work which spans national boundaries, more and more projects span national boundaries as well. In addition to the traditional concerns of scope, cost, time, and quality, the project management team must also consider the effect of time zone differences, national and regional holidays, travel requirements for face-to-face meetings, the logistics of teleconferencing, and often volatile political differences. With the new communication technologies some of these boundaries may have been reduced but the biggest problem that many organizations may face are cultural boundaries and the influences within these boundaries.

Cultural Influences

According to the American Heritage Dictionary of the English Language (1992) the culture is the "totality of socially transmitted behavior patterns, arts, beliefs, institutions, and all other products of human work and thought". Every project must operate within a context of one or more cultural norms. This area of influence includes political, economic, demographic, educational, ethical, ethnic, religious, and other areas of practice, belief, and attitudes that affect the way people and organizations interact. Most common problem that organizations face is lack of understanding multicultural concepts. Organizations need to have a basic knowledge of cultural diversities before business involvements. Exporting jobs to countries with different business and social culture will case many problems that will be costly to deal with in longer term. The best solution to understand cultural diversity is to educate employees.

DeSimone (1998) defines cultural diversity as "the existence of two or more persons from different cultural groups in any single group or organization". Most organizations are culturally diverse because their employees are from different cultural subgroups whether gender, race, ethnic origin. DeSimone, (1998) continues to explain that "even if an organization is culturally diverse, it may not be aware of or acknowledge the diversity". Diversity training programs vary in scope and length. At one extreme is one to three a day program for managers that are designed to transform them into culturally sensitive people. Most of these training programs are one-time programs that have no follow-up training to reinforce some of the issues.

According to Lynch, (1997) "there is some evidence suggesting that diversity training can at least make individuals aware of cultural distinction. A survey of employees who attended diversity training found that 62 percent felt the training was worthwhile in raising awareness of racial and genders differences. There were, however, most of the respondents whites, 87 percent and black, 52 percent felt that race relations were good or better in their own organization before the training". According to Tan (1996) "An organizational evaluation of a diversity training program at the Federal Aviation Administration (FAA) found that training made a significant difference in raising awareness".

CHAPTER 3

PROJECT MANAGEMENT PROCESSES

Project management is an integrative endeavor - an action, or failure to take action, in one area will usually affect other areas. The interactions may be straightforward and well-understood, or they may be subtle and uncertain. For example, a scope change will almost always affect project cost, but it may or may not affect team morale or product quality.

These interactions often require trade-offs among project objectives - performance in one area may be enhanced only by sacrificing performance in another.

Successful project management requires actively managing these interactions. To help in understanding the integrative nature of project management, and to emphasize the importance of integration, this book describes project management in terms of its component processes and their interactions. This chapter provides an introduction to the concept of project management as a number of interlinked processes and thus provides an essential foundation for understanding the process descriptions in Chapters 4 through 12. It includes the following major sections:

- Project Processes
- Process Groups
- Process Interactions
- Customizing Process Interactions

PROJECT PROCESSES

Projects are composed of processes. The American Heritage Dictionary of the English Language (1992) defines process as "A *process* is a series of actions bringing about a result". Project processes are performed by people and generally fall into one of two major categories:

1. *Project management processes* are concerned with describing and organizing the work of the project. The project management processes that are applicable to most projects, most of the time, are described briefly in this chapter and in detail in Chapters 4 through 12.
2. *Product-oriented processes* are concerned with specifying and creating the project product. Product-oriented processes are typically defined by the project life cycle (discussed in Chapter 2) and vary by application area.

Project management processes and product-oriented processes overlap and interact throughout the project. For example, the scope of the project cannot be defined in the absence of some basic understanding of how to create the product.

PROCESS GROUPS

Project management processes can be organized into five groups of one or more processes each:

1. Initiating Processes - recognizing that a project or phase should begin and committing to do so.

2. Planning Processes - devising and maintaining a workable scheme to accomplish the business need that the project was undertaken to address.
3. Executing Processes - coordinating people and other resources to carry out the plan.
4. Controlling Processes - ensuring that project objectives are met by monitoring and measuring progress and taking corrective action when necessary.
5. Closing Processes - formalizing acceptance of the project or phase and bringing it to an orderly end.

The process groups are linked by the results they produce the result or outcome of one becomes an input to another. Among the central process groups, the links are iterated planning provides executing with a documented project plan early on, and then provides documented updates to the plan as the project progresses. These connections are illustrated in Figure 3-1.

Figure 3-1. Links Among Process Groups in a Phase

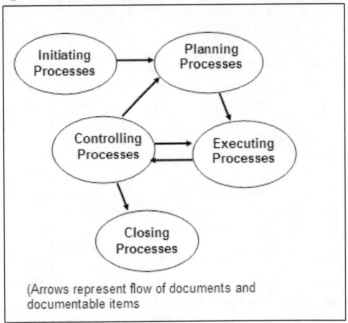

In addition, the project management process groups are not discrete, one-time events; they are overlapping activities which occur at varying levels of intensity throughout each phase of the project. Figure 3-2 illustrates how the process groups overlap and vary within a phase.

Figure 3-2. Overlap of Process Groups in a Phase

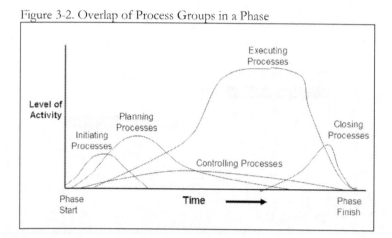

Finally, the process group interactions also cross phases such that closing one phase provides an input to initiating the next.

For example, closing a design phase requires customer acceptance of the design document. Simultaneously, the design document defines the product description for the ensuing implementation phase.

This interaction is illustrated in Figure 3-3. Repeating the initiation processes at the start of each phase helps to keep the project focused on the business need it was undertaken to address. It should also help ensure that the project is halted if the business need no longer exists or if the project is unlikely to satisfy that need. Business needs are discussed in more detail in the introduction to Chapter 5, Initiation.

Although Figure 3-3 is drawn with discrete phases and discrete processes, in an actual project there will be many overlaps.

Figure 3-3. Interaction Between Phases

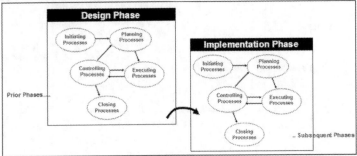

The planning process, for example, must not only provide details of the work to be done to bring the current phase of the project to successful completion but must also provide some preliminary description of work to be done in later phases. This progressive detailing of the project plan is often called *rolling wave planning*.

PROCESS INTERACTIONS

Within each process group, the individual processes are linked by their inputs and outputs. By focusing on these links, we can describe each process in terms of its:

- Inputs - documents or document-able items that will be acted upon.
- Tools and techniques - mechanisms applied to the inputs to create the outputs.
- Outputs - documents or document-able items that are a result of the process.

The project management processes common to most projects in most application areas are listed here and described in detail in Chapters 4 through 12. The numbers in parentheses after the process names identify the chapter and section where it is described. The process interactions illustrated here are also typical of most projects in most application areas. Chapter 3 discusses customizing both process descriptions and interactions.

Initiating Processes

Figure 3-4 illustrates the single process in this process group.

Figure 3-4. Relationships Among the Initiating Processes

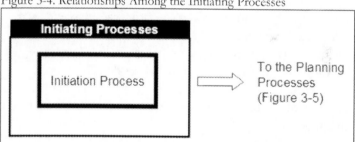

- Initiation committing the organization to begin the next phase of the project.

Planning Processes

Planning is of major importance to a project because the project involves doing something which has not been done before. As a result, there are relatively more processes in this section. However, the number of processes does not mean that project management is primarily planning, the amount of planning performed should be commensurate with the scope of the project and the usefulness of the information developed.

The relationships among the project planning processes are shown in Figure 3-5 (this chart is an explosion of the ellipse labeled "planning processes" in Figure 3-1).

These processes are subject to frequent iterations prior to completing the plan. For example, if the initial completion date is unacceptable, project resources, cost, or even scope may need to be redefined. In addition, planning is not an exact science-two different teams could generate very different plans for the same project.

Core processes. Some planning processes have clear dependencies that require them to be performed in essentially the same order on most projects. For example, activities must be defined before they can be scheduled or cost is estimated. These *core planning processes* may be iterated several times during any one phase of a project. They include:

- Scope Planning (chapter 5) - developing a written scope statement as the basis for future project decisions.
- Scope Definition (chapter 5) - subdividing the major project deliverables into smaller, more manageable components.
- Activity Definition (chapter 6) - identifying the specific activities that must be performed to produce the various project deliverables.

Figure 3-5. Relationships Among the Planning Processes

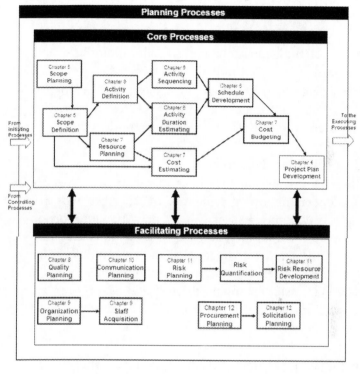

- Activity Sequencing (chapter 6) - identifying and documenting interactivity dependencies.

- Activity Duration Estimating (chapter 6) - estimating the number of work periods which will be needed to complete individual activities.

- Schedule Development (chapter 6) - analyzing activity sequences, activity durations, and resource requirements to create the project schedule.

- Resource Planning (chapter 7) - determining what resources (people, equipment, materials) and what quantities of each should be used to perform project activities.

- Cost Estimating (chapter 7) - developing an approximation (estimate) of the costs of the resources needed to complete project activities.
- Cost Budgeting (chapter 7) - allocating the overall cost estimate to individual work items.
- Project Plan Development (chapter 4) - taking the results of other planning processes and putting them into a consistent and coherent document.

Facilitating Processes

Interactions among the other planning processes are more dependent on the nature of the project. For example, on some projects there may be little or no identifiable risk until after most of the planning has been done and the team recognizes that the cost and schedule targets are extremely aggressive and thus involve considerable risk. Although these *facilitating processes* are performed intermittently and as needed during project planning, they are not optional. They include:

- Quality Planning (chapter 8)-identifying which quality standards are relevant to the project and determining how to satisfy them.
- Organizational Planning (chapter 9) - identifying, documenting, and assigning project roles, responsibilities, and reporting relationships.
- Staff Acquisition (chapter 9) - getting the human resources needed assigned to and working on the project.
- Communications Planning (chapter 10) - determining the information and communications needs of the stakeholders: who needs what information, when will they need it, and how will it be given to them.

- Risk Identification (chapter 11) - determining which risks are likely to affect the project and documenting the characteristics of each.
- Risk Quantification (chapter 11) - evaluating risks and risk interactions to assess the range of possible project outcomes.
- Risk Response Development (chapter 11) - defining enhancement steps for opportunities and responses to threats.
- Procurement Planning (chapter 12) - determining what to procure and when.
- Solicitation Planning (chapter 12) - documenting product requirements and identifying potential sources.

Executing Processes

The executing processes include core processes and facilitating processes as described in Chapter 3, Planning Processes. Figure 3-6 illustrates how the following processes interact:

- Project Plan Execution (chapter 4) - carrying out the project plan by performing the activities included therein.
- Scope Verification (chapter 5) - formalizing acceptance of the project scope.
- Quality Assurance (chapter 5) - evaluating overall project performance on a regular basis to provide confidence that the project will satisfy the relevant quality standards.
- Team Development (chapter 9) - developing individual and group skills to enhance project performance.

- Information Distribution (chapter 10) - making needed information available to project stakeholders in a timely manner.
- Solicitation (chapter 12) - obtaining quotations, bids, offers, or proposals as appropriate.
- Source Selection (chapter 12) - choosing from among potential sellers.
- Contract Administration (chapter 12) - managing the relationship with the seller.

Figure 3-6. Relationships Among the Executing Processes

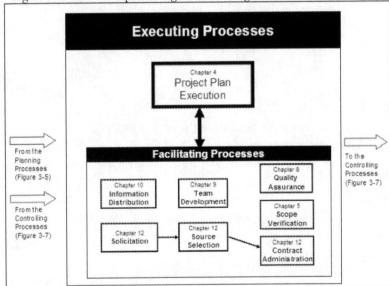

Controlling Processes

Project performance must be measured regularly to identify variances from the plan.

Variances are fed into the control processes in the various knowledge areas. To the extent that significant variances are observed (i.e., those that jeopardize the project objectives), adjustments to the plan are made by repeating the appropriate project planning processes. For example, a missed activity finish date may require adjustments to the current staffing plan, reliance on overtime, or trade-offs between budget and schedule objectives. Controlling also includes taking preventive action in anticipation of possible problems.

The controlling process group contains core processes and facilitating processes as described in Chapter 3, Planning Processes.

Figure 3-7 illustrates how the following processes interact:

- Overall Change Control (chapter 4) - coordinating changes across the entire project.
- Scope Change Control (chapter 5) - controlling changes to project scope.
- Schedule Control (chapter 6) - controlling changes to the project schedule.
- Cost Control (chapter 7) - controlling changes to the project budget.
- Quality Control (chapter 8) - monitoring specific project results to determine if they comply with relevant quality standards and identifying ways to eliminate causes of unsatisfactory performance.
- Performance Reporting (chapter 10) - collecting and disseminating performance information. This includes status reporting, progress measurement, and forecasting.
- Risk Response Control (chapter 11) - responding to changes in risk over the course of the project.

Figure 3-7. Relationships Among the Controlling Processes

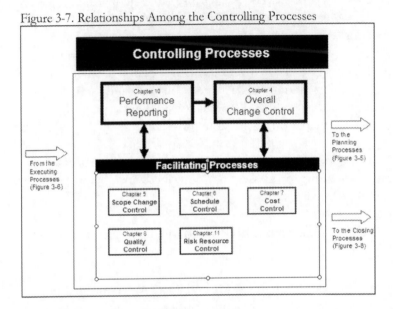

Closing Processes

Figure 3-8 illustrates how the following processes interact:

Figure 3-8. Relationships Among the Closing Processes

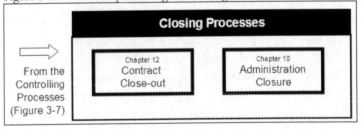

- Administrative Closure (Chapter 10) - generating, gathering, and disseminating information to formalize phase or project completion.

- Contract Close-out (Chapter 12) - completion and settlement of the contract, including resolution of any open items.

CUSTOMIZING PROCESS INTERACTIONS

The processes identified and the interactions illustrated in Chapter 3 meet the test of general acceptance, they apply to most projects most of the time. However, not all of the processes will be needed on all projects, and not all of the interactions will apply to all projects. For example:

- An organization that makes extensive use of contractors may explicitly describe where in the planning process each procurement process occurs.
- The absence of a process does not mean that it should not be performed. The project management team should identify and manage all the processes that are needed to ensure a successful project.
- Projects which are dependent on unique resources (commercial software development, biopharmaceuticals, etc.) may define roles and responsibilities prior to scope definition since what can be done may be a function of who will be available to do it.
- Some process outputs may be predefined as constraints. For example, management may specify a target completion date rather than allowing it to be determined by the planning process.

- Larger projects may need relatively more detail. For example, risk identification might be further subdivided to focus separately on identifying cost risks, schedule risks, technical risks, and quality risks.
- On subprojects and smaller projects, relatively little effort will be spent on processes whose outputs have been defined at the project level (e.g., a subcontractor may ignore risks explicitly assumed by the prime contractor) or on processes that provide only marginal utility (there may be no formal communications plan on a four-person project).

When there is a need to make a change, the change should be clearly identified, carefully evaluated, and actively managed.

CHAPTER 4

PROJECT INTEGRATION MANAGEMENT

Project Integration Management includes the processes required to ensure that the various elements of the project are properly coordinated. It involves making tradeoffs among competing objectives and alternatives in order to meet or exceed stakeholder needs and expectations. While all project management processes are integrative to some extent, the processes described in this chapter are *primarily* integrative. Figure 4-1 provides an overview of the following major processes:

- Project Plan Development - taking the results of other planning processes and putting them into a consistent, coherent document.
- Project Plan Execution - carrying out the project plan by performing the activities included therein.
- Overall Change Control - coordinating changes across the entire project.

Figure 4-1. Project Integration Management Overview

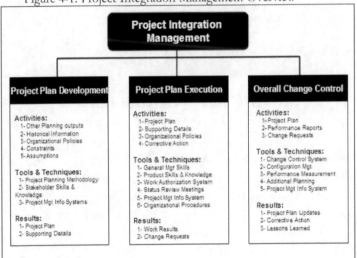

These processes interact with each other and with the processes in the other knowledge areas as well. Each process may involve effort from one or more individuals or groups of individuals based on the needs of the project. Each process generally occurs at least once in every project phase.

Although the processes are presented here as discrete elements with well-defined interfaces, in practice they may overlap and interact in ways not detailed here. Process interactions are discussed in detail in Chapter 3.

The processes, tools, and techniques used to integrate *project management* processes are the focus of this chapter. For example, project integration management comes into play when a cost estimate is needed for a contingency plan or when risks associated with various staffing alternatives must be identified. However, for a project to be completed successfully, integration must also occur in a number of other areas as well. For example:

- The work of the project must be integrated with the ongoing operations of the performing organization.
- Product scope and project scope must be integrated (the difference between product and project scope is discussed in the introduction to Chapter 5).
- Deliverables from different functional specialties (such as civil, electrical, and mechanical drawings for an engineering design project) must be integrated.

PROJECT PLAN DEVELOPMENT

Project plan development uses the outputs of the other planning processes to create a consistent, coherent document that can be used to guide both project execution and project control. This process is almost always iterated several times. For example, the initial draft may include generic resources and undated durations while the final plan reflects specific resources and explicit dates. The project plan is used to:

- Guide project execution.
- Document project planning assumptions.
- Document project planning decisions regarding alternatives chosen.
- Facilitate communication among stakeholders.
- Define key management reviews as to content, extent, and timing.

- Provide a baseline for progress measurement and project control.

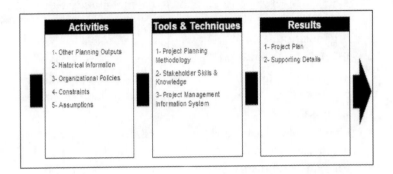

Activities	Tools & Techniques	Results
1- Other Planning Outputs 2- Historical Information 3- Organizational Policies 4- Constraints 5- Assumptions	1- Project Planning Methodology 2- Stakeholder Skills & Knowledge 3- Project Management Information System	1- Project Plan 2- Supporting Details

Activities for Project Plan Development
1- Other Planning Outputs

All of the outputs of the planning process in the other knowledge areas (Chapter 3 provides a summary of these project planning processes) are inputs to developing the project plan. Other planning outputs include both base documents such as the work breakdown structure as well as the supporting detail.

Many projects will also require application area-specific inputs (e.g., most construction projects will require a cash flow forecast).

2- Historical Information

The available historical information (e.g., estimating databases, records of past project performance) should have been consulted during the other project planning processes. This information should also be available during project plan development to assist with verifying assumptions and assessing alternatives that are identified as part of this process.

3- Organizational Policies

Any and all of the organizations involved in the project may have formal and informal policies whose effects must be considered. Organizational policies which typically must be considered include, but are not limited to:

- Quality Management - process audits, continuous improvement targets.
- Personnel Administration - hiring and firing guidelines, employee performance reviews.
- Financial Controls - time reporting, required expenditure and disbursement reviews, accounting codes, standard contract provisions.

4- Constraints

Constraints are factors that will limit the project management team's options. For example, a predefined budget is a constraint that is highly likely to limit the team's options regarding scope, staffing, and schedule. When a project is performed under contract, contractual provisions will generally be constraints.

5- Assumptions

Assumptions are factors that, for planning purposes, will be considered to be true, real, or certain. For example, if the date that a key person will become available is uncertain, the team may assume a specific start date. Assumptions generally involve a degree of risk.

Tools and Techniques for Project Plan Envelopment

1- Project Planning Methodology

A project planning methodology is any structured approach used to guide the project team during development of the project plan. It may be as simple as standard forms and templates (whether paper or electronic, formal or informal) or as complex as a series of required simulations (e.g., Monte Carlo analysis of schedule risk). Most project planning methodologies make use of a combination of "hard" tools such as project management software and "soft" tools such as facilitated start-up meetings.

2- Stakeholder Skills and Knowledge

Every stakeholder has skills and knowledge which may be useful in developing the project plan. The project management team must create an environment in which the stakeholders can contribute appropriately (see also Chapter 9, Team Development). Who contributes, what they contribute, and when will vary. For example:

- On a construction project being done under a lump sum contract, the professional cost engineer will make a major contribution to the profitability objective during proposal preparation when the contract amount, is being determined.
- On a project where staffing is defined in advance, the individual contributors may contribute significantly to meeting cost and schedule objectives by reviewing duration and effort estimates for reasonableness.

3- Project Management Information System (PMIS)

A project management information system consists of the tools and techniques used to gather, integrate, and disseminate the outputs of the other project management processes. It is used to support all aspects of the project from initiating through closing and generally includes both manual and automated systems.

Results from Project Plan Development

1- Project Plan

The project plan is a formal, approved document used to manage and control project execution. It should be distributed as defined in the communications management plan (e.g., management of the performing organization may require broad coverage with little detail, while a contractor may require complete details on a single subject). In some application areas, the term *integrated project plan* is used to refer to this document.

A clear distinction should be made between the project plan and the project performance measurement baselines. The project plan is a document or collection of documents that should be expected to change over time as more information becomes available about the project. The performance measurement baselines represent a *management control* that will generally change only intermittently and then generally only in response to an approved scope change.

There are many ways to organize and present the project plan, but it commonly includes all of the following

- Project charter.
- A description of the project management approach or strategy (a summary of the individual management plans from the other knowledge areas).
- Scope statement, which includes the project deliverables and the project objectives.
- Work Breakdown Structure (WBS) to the level at which control will be exercised.
- Cost estimates, scheduled start dates, and responsibility assignments to the level of the WBS at which control will be exercised.
- Performance measurement baselines for schedule and cost.
- Major milestones and target dates for each.
- Key or required staff.
- Key risks, including constraints and assumptions, and planned responses for each.
- Subsidiary management plans, including scope management plan, schedule management plan, etc.
- Open issues and pending decisions.

Other project planning outputs should be included in the formal plan based upon the needs of the individual project. For example, the project plan for a large project will generally include a project organization chart.

2- Supporting Detail
Supporting detail for the project plan includes:

- Outputs from other planning processes that are not included in the project plan.

- Additional information or documentation generated during development of the project plan (e.g., constraints and assumptions that were not previously known).
- Technical documentation such as requirements, specifications, and designs.
- Documentation of relevant standards.

This material should be organized as needed to facilitate its use during project plan execution.

PROJECT PLAN EXECUTION

Project plan execution is the primary process for carrying out the project plan - the vast majority of the project's budget will be expended in performing this process. In this process, the project manager and the project management team must coordinate and direct the various technical and organizational interfaces that exist in the project.

It is the project process that is most directly affected by the project application area in that the product of the project is actually created here.

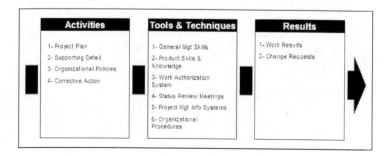

Activities to Project Plan Execution

1- Project Plan

The project plan is described in Chapter 4. The subsidiary management plans (scope management plan, risk management plan, procurement management plan, etc.) and the performance measurement baselines are key inputs to project plan execution.

2- Supporting Detail

Supporting detail is described in Chapter 4.

3- Organizational Policies

Organizational policies are described in Chapter 4. Any and all of the organizations involved in the project may have formal and informal policies which may affect project plan execution.

4- Corrective Action

Corrective action is anything done to bring expected future project performance into line with the project plan. Corrective action is an output of the various control processes - it completes the feedback loop needed to ensure effective project management.

Tools and Techniques for Project Plan Execution

1- General Management Skills

General management skills such as leadership, communicating, and negotiating are essential to effective project plan execution. General management skills are described in Chapter 2.

2- Product Skills and Knowledge

The project team must have access to an appropriate set of skills and knowledge about the project product. The necessary skills are defined as part of planning (especially in resource planning, Chapter 7) and are provided through the staff acquisition process (described in Chapter 9).

3- Work Authorization System

A work authorization system is a formal procedure for sanctioning project work to ensure that work is done at the right time and in the proper sequence. The primary mechanism is typically a written authorization to begin work on a specific activity or work package.

The design of a work authorization system should balance the value of the control provided with the cost of that control. For example, on many ·smaller projects, verbal authorizations will be adequate.

4- Status Review Meetings

Status review meetings are regularly scheduled meetings held to exchange information about the project. On most projects, status review meetings will be held at various frequencies and on different levels (e.g., the project management team may meet weekly by itself and monthly with the customer).

5- Project Management Information System

The project management information system is described in Chapter 4.

6- Organizational Procedures

Any and all of the organizations involved in the project may have formal and informal procedures useful during project execution.

Results from Project Plan Execution

1- Work Results

Work results are the outcomes of the activities performed to accomplish the project. Information on work results which deliverables have been completed and which have not, to what extent quality standards are being met, what costs have been incurred or committed, etc. is collected as part of project plan execution and fed into the performance reporting process (see Chapter 10 for a more detailed discussion of performance reporting).

2- Change Requests

Change requests (e.g., to expand or contract project scope, to modify cost or schedule estimates, etc.) are often identified while the work of the project is being done.

OVERALL CHANGE CONTROL

Overall change control is concerned with (a) influencing the factors which create changes to ensure that changes are beneficial, (b) determining that a change has occurred, and (c) managing the actual changes when and as they occur. Overall change control requires:

- Maintaining the integrity of the performance measurement baselines - all approved changes should be reflected in the project plan, but only project scope changes will affect the performance measurement baselines.

- Ensuring that changes to the product scope are reflected in the definition of the project scope (the difference between product and project scope is discussed in the introduction to Chapter 5).

- Coordinating changes across knowledge areas as illustrated in Figure 4-2.

Figure 4-2. Coordinating Changes Across the Entire Project

```
┌─────────────────────────────────────────────────────┐
│  ┌────────────────────┐      ┌────────────────────┐  │
│  │    Performance     │ ──▶  │      Overall       │  │
│  │     Reporting      │      │   Change Control   │  │
│  └────────────────────┘      └────────────────────┘  │
│            ▲▼                          ▲▼            │
│  ┌─────────────────────────────────────────────────┐ │
│  │         Subsidiary Change Control               │ │
│  │                                                 │ │
│  │   • Scope Change Control                        │ │
│  │   • Schedule Change Control                     │ │
│  │   • Cost Change Control                         │ │
│  │   • Quality Control                             │ │
│  │   • Risk Change Control                         │ │
│  │   • Contract Administration                     │ │
│  └─────────────────────────────────────────────────┘ │
└─────────────────────────────────────────────────────┘
```

- For example, a proposed schedule change will often affect cost, risk, quality, and staffing.

Activities to Overall Change Control

1- Project Plan
The project plan provides the baseline against which changes will be controlled (see Chapter 4).

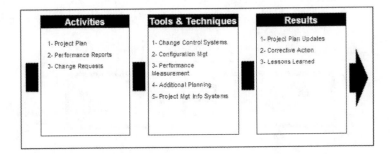

2- Performance Reports
Performance reports (described in Chapter 10) provide information on project performance. Performance reports may also alert the project team to issues which may cause problems in the future.

3- Change Requests
Change requests may occur in many forms oral or written, direct or indirect, externally or internally initiated, and legally mandated or optional.

Tools and Techniques for Overall Change Control

1- Change Control System
A change control system is a collection of formal, documented procedures that defines the steps by which

official project documents may be changed. It includes the paperwork, tracking systems, and approval levels necessary for authorizing changes.

In many cases, the performing organization will have a change control system that can be adopted "as is" for use by the project. However, if an appropriate system is not available, the project management team will need to develop one as part of the project.

Many change control systems include a Change Control Board (CCB) responsible for approving or rejecting change requests. The powers and responsibilities of a CCB should be well-defined and agreed upon by key stakeholders. On large, complex projects, there may be multiple CCBs with different responsibilities.

The change control system must also include procedures to handle changes which may be approved without prior review; for example, as the result of emergencies. Typically, a change control system will allow for "automatic" approval of defined categories of changes. These changes must still be documented and captured so that they do not cause problems later in the project.

2- *Configuration Management*
Configuration management is any documented procedure used to apply technical and administrative direction and surveillance to:

- Identify and document the functional and physical characteristics of an item or system.
- Control any changes to such characteristics.
- Record and report the change and its implementation status.

- Audit the items and system to verify conformance to requirements.

In many application areas, configuration management is a subset of the change control system and is used to ensure that the description of the project product is correct and complete. However, in some application areas, the term *configuration management* is used to describe any rigorous change control system.

3- Performance Measurement
Performance measurement techniques such as earned value (described in Chapter 10) help to assess whether variances from the plan require corrective action.

4- Additional Planning
Projects seldom run exactly according to plan. Prospective changes may require new or revised cost estimates, modified activity sequences, analysis of risk response alternatives, or other adjustments to the project plan.

5- Project Management Information System
Project management information systems are described in Chapter 4.

Results from Overall Change Control

1- Project Plan Updates
Project plan updates are any modification to the contents of the project plan or the supporting detail (described in Chapter 4, respectively). Appropriate stakeholders must be notified as needed.

2- Corrective Action

Corrective action is described in Chapter 4.

3- Lessons Learned

The causes of variances, the reasoning behind the corrective action chosen, and other types of lessons learned should be documented so that they become part of the historical database for both this project and other projects of the performing organization.

CHAPTER 5

PROJECT SCOPE MANAGEMENT

Turner (1992) defines "Project Scope Management includes the processes required to ensure that the project includes all the work required, and only the work required, to complete the project successfully". It is primarily concerned with defining and controlling what is or is not included in the project. Figure 5-1 provides an overview of the major project scope management processes:

- Initiation - committing the organization to begin the next phase of the project.
- Scope Planning - developing a written scope statement as the basis for future project decisions.
- Scope Definition - subdividing the major project deliverables into smaller, more manageable components.
- Scope Verification - formalizing acceptance of the project scope.
- Scope Change Control - controlling changes to project scope.

Figure 5-1. Project Scope Management Overview

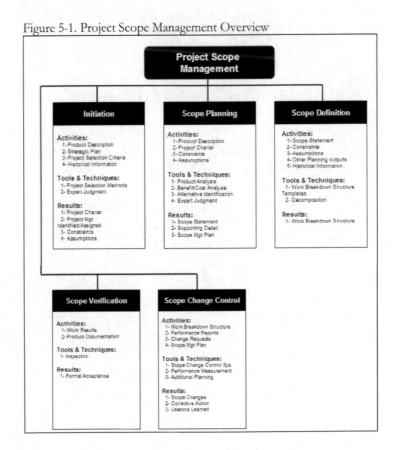

These processes interact with each other and with the processes in the other process areas as well. Each process may involve effort from one or more individuals or groups of individuals based on the needs of the project. Each process generally occurs at least once in every project phase.

Although the processes are presented here as discrete elements with well-defined interfaces, in practice they may overlap and interact in ways not detailed here.

Process interactions are discussed in detail in Chapter 3.

In the project context, the term "scope" may refer to:

- Product scope - the features and functions that are to be included in a product or service.
- Project scope - the work that must be done in order to deliver a product with the specified features and functions.

The processes, tools and techniques used to manage *project* scope are the focus of this chapter. The processes, tools, and techniques used to manage *product* scope vary by application area and are usually defined as part of the project life cycle (the project life cycle is discussed in Chapter 2).

A project consists of a single product, but that product may include subsidiary elements, each with their own separate but interdependent product scopes. For example, a new telephone system would generally include four subsidiary elements hardware, software, training, and implementation.

Completion of the *product* scope is measured against the requirements while completion of the *project* scope is measured against the plan. Both types of scope management must be well integrated to ensure that the work of the project will result in delivery of the specified product.

INITIATION

Initiation is the process of formally recognizing that a new project exists or that an existing project should continue into its next phase (see Chapter 2 for a more detailed discussion of project phases). This formal initiation links the project to the ongoing work of the performing organization. In some organizations, a project is not formally initiated until after completion of a feasibility study, a preliminary plan, or some other equivalent form of analysis which was itself separately initiated. Some types of projects, especially internal service projects and new product development projects are initiated informally and some limited amount of work is done in order to secure the approvals needed for formal initiation. Projects are typically authorized as a result of one or more of the following:

- A market demand (e.g., an oil company authorizes a project to build a new refinery in response to chronic gasoline shortages).
- A business need (e.g., a training company authorizes a project to create a new course in order to increase its revenues).
- A customer request (e.g., an electric utility authorizes a project to build a new substation to serve a new industrial park).
- A technological advance (e.g., an electronics firm authorizes a new project to develop a video game player after the introduction of the video cassette recorder).
- A legal requirement (e.g., a paint manufacturer authorizes a project to establish guidelines for the handling of toxic materials). These stimuli may

also be called problems, opportunities, or business requirements.

The central theme of all these terms is that management generally must make a decision about how to respond.

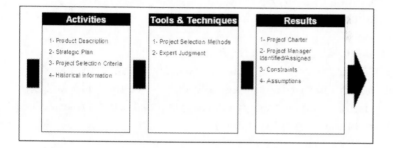

Activities to Initiation
1- Product Description

The product description documents the characteristics of the product or service that the project was undertaken to create. The product description will generally have less detail in early phases and more detail in later ones as the product characteristics are progressively elaborated.

The product description should also document the relationship between the product or service being created and the business need or other stimulus that gave rise to the project. While the form and substance of the product description will vary, it should always be detailed enough to support later project planning.

Many projects involve one organization (the seller) doing work under contract to another (the buyer). In such circumstances, the initial product description is usually provided by the buyer. If the buyer's work is itself a project, the buyer's product description is a statement of work as described in Chapter 12.

2- Strategic Plan

All projects should be supportive of the performing organization's strategic goals - the strategic plan of the performing organization should be considered as a factor in project selection decisions.

3- Project Selection Criteria

Project selection criteria are typically defined in terms of the product of the project and can cover the full range of possible management concerns (financial return, market share, public perceptions, etc.).

4- Historical Information

Historical information about both the results of previous project selection decisions and previous project performance should be considered to the extent it is available. When initiation involves approval for the next phase of a project, information about the results of previous phases is often critical.

Tools and Techniques for Initiation

1- Project Selection Methods

According to Iyigiin (1993) project selection methods generally fall into one of two broad categories:

1. "Benefit measurement methods - comparative approaches, scoring models, benefit contribution, or economic models.

2. Constrained optimization methods - mathematical models using linear, nonlinear, dynamic, integer, and multi-objective programming algorithms".

These methods are often referred to as *decision models.* Decision models include generalized techniques (decision trees, forced choice, and others) as well as specialized ones (Analytic Hierarchy Process, Logical Framework Analysis, and others). Applying complex project selection criteria in a sophisticated model is often treated as a separate project phase.

2- Expert Judgment

Expert judgment will often be required to assess the inputs to this process. Such expertise may be provided by any group or individual with specialized knowledge or training and is available from many sources including:

- Other units within the performing organization
- Consultants
- Professional and technical associations
- Industry groups

Results from Initiation

1- Project Charter

A project charter is a document that formally recognizes the existence of a project. It should include, either directly or by reference to other documents:

- The business need that the project was undertaken to address.
- The product description (described in Chapter 5).

The project charter should be issued by a manager external to the project and at a level appropriate to the needs of the project. It provides the project manager with the authority to apply organizational resources to project activities.

When a project is performed under contract, the signed contract will generally serve as the project charter for the seller.

2- Project Manager Identified/Assigned

In general, the project manager should be identified and assigned as early in the project as is feasible. The project manager should always be assigned prior to the start of project plan execution (described in Chapter 4) and preferably before much project planning has been done (the project planning processes are described in Chapter 3).

3- Constraints

Constraints are factors that will limit the project management team's options. For example, a predefined budget is a constraint that is highly likely to limit the team's options regarding scope, staffing, and schedule. When a project is performed under contract, contractual provisions will generally be constraints.

4- Assumptions

Assumptions are factors that, for planning purposes, will be considered to be true, real, or certain. For example, if the date that a key person will become available is uncertain, the team may assume a specific start date. Assumptions generally involve a degree of risk. They may be identified here or they may be an output of risk identification (described in Chapter 11).

SCOPE PLANNING

Scope planning is the process of developing a written scope statement as the basis for future project decisions including, in particular, the criteria used to determine if the project or phase has been completed successfully. A written scope statement is necessary for both projects and subprojects. For example, an engineering firm contracted to design a petroleum processing plant must have a scope statement defining the boundaries of its work on the design subproject. The scope statement forms the basis for an agreement between the project team and the project customer by identifying both the project objectives and the major project deliverables.

If all the elements of the scope statement are already available (e.g., a request for proposal may identify the major deliverables, the project charter may define the project objectives), this process may involve little more than physically creating the written document.

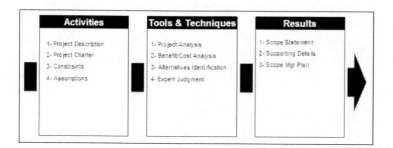

Activities to Scope Planning

1- Product Description
The product description is discussed in Chapter 5.

2- Project Charter
The project charter is described in Chapter 5.

3- Constraints
Constraints are described in Chapter 5.

4- Assumptions
Assumptions are described in Chapter 5.

Tools and Techniques for Scope Planning

1- Product Analysis
Product analysis involves developing a better understanding of the product of the project. It includes techniques such as systems engineering, value engineering, value analysis, function analysis, and quality function deployment.

2- Benefit/Cost Analysis
Benefit/cost analysis involves estimating tangible and intangible costs (outlays) and benefits (returns) of various project alternatives, and then using financial measures such as return on investment or payback period to assess the relative desirability of the identified alternatives.

3- Alternatives Identification
This is a catchall term for any technique used to generate different approaches to the project. There are a variety of general management techniques often used here, the most common of which are brainstorming and lateral thinking.

4- Expert Judgment

Expert judgment is described in Chapter 5.

Results from Scope Planning

1- Scope Statement

The scope statement provides a documented basis for making future project decisions and for confirming or developing common understanding of project scope among the stakeholders. As the project progresses, the scope statement may need to be revised or refined to reflect changes to the scope of the project.

The scope statement should include, either directly or by reference to other documents:

- Project justification - the business need that the project was undertaken to address. The project justification provides the basis for evaluating future trade-offs.
- Project product - a brief summary of the product description (the product description is discussed in Chapter 5).
- Project deliverables - a list of the summary level sub-products whose full and satisfactory delivery marks completion of the project. For example, the major deliverables for a software development project might include the working computer code, a user manual, and an interactive tutorial. When known, exclusions should be identified, but anything not explicitly included is implicitly excluded.
- Project objectives - the quantifiable criteria that must be met for the project to be considered successful. Project objectives must include, at least,

cost, schedule, and quality measures. Project objectives should have an attribute (e.g., cost), a yardstick (e.g., U.S. dollars), and an absolute or relative value (e.g., less than 1.5 million). Un-quantified objectives (e.g., "customer satisfaction") entail high risk.

In some application areas, project deliverables are called project objectives while project objectives are called critical success factors.

2- Supporting Detail

Supporting detail for the scope statement should be documented and organized as needed to facilitate its use by other project management processes. Supporting detail should always include documentation of all identified assumptions and constraints. The amount of additional detail varies by application area.

3- Scope Management Plan

This book describes how project scope will be managed and how scope changes will be integrated into the project. It should also include an assessment of the expected stability of the project scope (i.e., how likely is it to change, how frequently, and by how much). The scope management plan should also include a clear description of how scope changes will be identified and classified (this is particularly difficult and therefore absolutely essential when the product characteristics are still being elaborated).

A scope management plan may be formal or informal, highly detailed or broadly framed based on the needs of the project. It is a subsidiary element of the overall project plan (described in Chapter 4).

SCOPE DEFINITION

Scope definition involves subdividing the major project deliverables (as identified in the scope statement) into smaller, more manageable components in order to:

- Improve the accuracy of cost, time, and resource estimates.
- Define a baseline for performance measurement and control.
- Facilitate clear responsibility assignments.

According to "Scope Definition and Control Publication" (1986) the proper scope definition is critical to project success. "When there is poor scope definition, final project costs can be expected to be higher because of the inevitable changes which disrupt project rhythm, cause rework, increase project time, and lower the productivity and morale of the workforce".

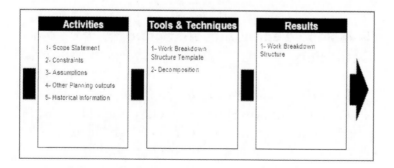

Activities	Tools & Techniques	Results
1- Scope Statement 2- Constraints 3- Assumptions 4- Other Planning outputs 5- Historical Information	1- Work Breakdown Structure Template 2- Decomposition	1- Work Breakdown Structure

Activities to Scope Definition

1- Scope Statement
The scope statement is described in Chapter 5.

2- Constraints
Constraints are described in Chapter 5. When a project is done under contract, the constraints defined by contractual provisions are often important considerations during scope definition.

3- Assumptions
Assumptions are described in Chapter 5.

4- Other planning outputs
The outputs of the processes in other areas should be reviewed for possible impact on project scope definition.

5- Historical information
Historical information about previous projects should be considered during scope definition. Information about errors and omissions on previous projects should be especially useful.

Tools and Techniques for Scope Definition

1- Work Breakdown Structure Templates.
A Work Breakdown Structure (WBS), (described in Chapter 5) from a previous project can often be used as a template for a new project. Although each project is unique, WBSs can often be "reused" since most projects will resemble another project to some extent. For example, most projects within a given organization will have the

same or similar project life cycles and will thus have the same or similar deliverables required from each phase.

Many application areas have standard or semi-standard WBSs that can be used as templates. For example, the U.S. Department of Defense has defined standard WBSs for Defense Materiel Items. A portion of one of these templates is shown as Figure 5-2.

Figure 5-2. Sample Work Breakdown Structure for Defense Material Items

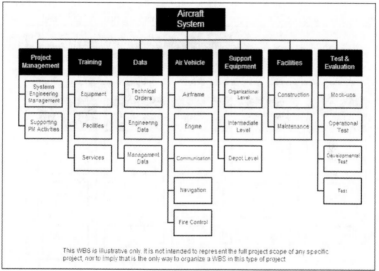

2- Decomposition

Decomposition involves subdividing the major project deliverables into smaller, more manageable components until the deliverables are defined in sufficient detail to support future project activities (planning, executing, controlling, and closing). Decomposition involves the following major steps:

(Step 1) Identify the major elements of the project. In general, the major elements will be the project deliverables and project management. However, the major elements should always be defined in terms of how the project will actually be managed. For example:

- The phases of the project life cycle may be used as the first level of decomposition with the project deliverables repeated at the second level, as illustrated in Figure 5-3.

Figure 5-3. Sample Work Breakdown Structure Organized by Phase

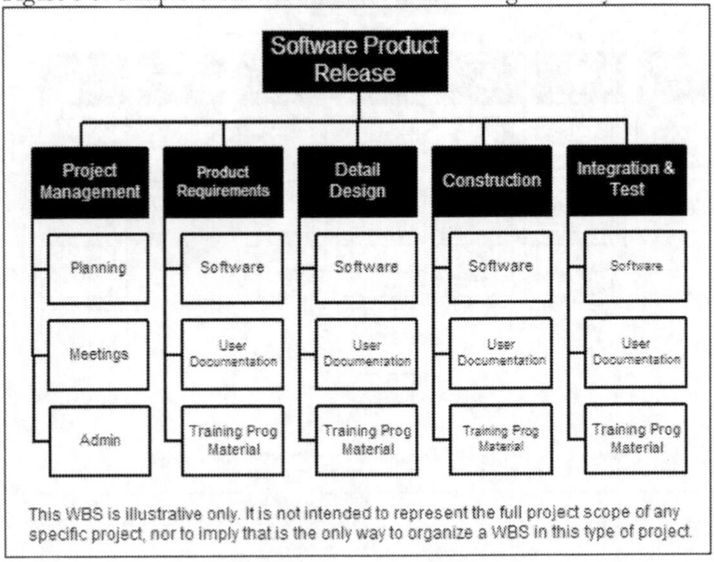

This WBS is illustrative only. It is not intended to represent the full project scope of any specific project, nor to imply that is the only way to organize a WBS in this type of project.

- The organizing principle within each branch of the WBS may vary, as illustrated in Figure 5-4.

Figure 5-4. Sample Work Breakdown Structure for Waste Water
Treatment Plant

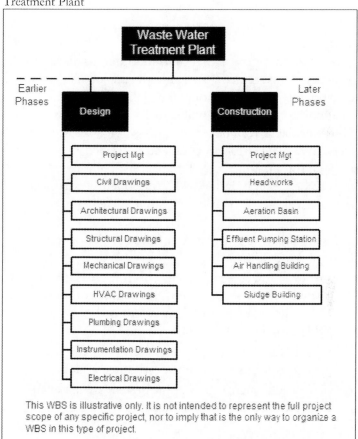

(Step 2) Decide if adequate cost and duration estimates
can be developed at this level of detail for each element.
The meaning of *adequate* may change over the course of
the project-decomposition of a deliverable that will be
produced far in the future may not be possible. For each
element, proceed to Step 4 if there is adequate detail and

to Step 3 if there is not. This means that different elements may have differing levels of decomposition.

(Step 3) Identify constituent elements of the deliverable. Constituent elements should be described in terms of tangible, verifiable results in order to facilitate performance measurement. As with the major elements, the constituent elements should be defined in terms of how the work of the project will actually be accomplished. Tangible, verifiable results can include services as well as products (e.g., *status reporting* could be described as *weekly status reports;* for a manufactured item, constituent elements might include several individual components plus *final assembly*). Repeat Step 2 on each constituent element.

(Step 4) Verify the correctness of the decomposition:

- Are the lower level items both necessary and sufficient for completion of the item decomposed? If not, the constituent elements must be modified (added to, deleted from, or redefined).
- Is each item clearly and completely defined? If not, the descriptions must be revised or expanded.
- Can each item be appropriately scheduled? Budgeted?

Assigned to a specific organizational unit (e.g., department, team, or person) who will accept responsibility for satisfactory completion. Of the item? If not, revisions are needed to provide adequate management control.

Results from Scope Definition

1- Work Breakdown Structure (WBS)

A Work Breakdown Structure (WBS) is a deliverable-oriented grouping of project elements that organizes and defines the total scope of the project:

Work not in the WBS is outside the scope of the project. As with the scope statement, the WBS is often used to develop or confirm a common understanding of project scope. Each descending level represents an increasingly detailed description of the project elements. Chapter 5 describes the most common approach for developing a WBS.

A WBS is normally presented in chart form as illustrated in Figures 5-2, 5-3, and 5-4 (previous pages); however, the WBS should not be confused with the method of presentation drawing an unstructured activity list in chart form does not make it a WBS.

Each item in the WBS is generally assigned a unique identifier; these identifiers are often known collectively as the *code of accounts*. The items at the lowest level of the WBS are often referred to as *work packages*. These work packages may be further decomposed as described in Chapter 6, Activity Definition.

Work element descriptions are often collected in a *WBS dictionary*. A WBS dictionary will typically include work package descriptions as well as other planning information such as schedule dates, cost budgets, and staff assignments.

The WBS should not be confused with other kinds of "breakdown" structures used to present project information. Other structures commonly used in some application areas include:

- Contractual Work Breakdown Structure (CWBS), which is used to define the level of reporting that the seller will provide the buyer. The CWBS generally includes less detail than the WBS used by the seller to manage the seller's work.
- Organizational Breakdown Structure (OBS), which is used to show which work elements have been assigned to which organizational units.
- Resource Breakdown Structure (RBS), which is a variation of the OBS and is typically used when work elements are assigned to individuals.
- Bill of Materials (BOM), which presents a hierarchical view of the physical assemblies, subassemblies, and components needed to fabricate a manufactured product.
- Project Breakdown Structure (PBS), which is fundamentally the same as a properly done WBS. The term PBS is widely used in application areas where the term WBS is incorrectly used to refer to a BOM.

SCOPE VERIFICATION

Scope verification is the process of formalizing acceptance of the project scope by the stakeholders (sponsor, client, customer, etc.). It requires reviewing work products and results to ensure that all were completed correctly and satisfactorily. If the project is terminated early, the scope verification process should establish and document the level and extent of completion. Scope verification differs from quality control (described in Chapter 8) in that it is primarily concerned with *acceptance* of the work results while quality control is primarily concerned with the *correctness* of the work results.

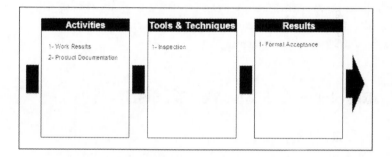

Activities to Scope Verification

1- Work Results

Work results which deliverables have been fully or partially completed, what costs have been incurred or committed, etc. are an output of project plan execution (discussed in Chapter 4).

2- Product Documentation

Documents produced to describe the project's products must be available for review. The terms used to describe this documentation (plans, specifications, technical documentation, drawings, etc.) vary by application area.

Tools and Techniques for Scope Verification

1- Inspection

Inspection includes activities such as measuring, examining, and testing undertaken to determine whether results conform to requirements. Inspections are variously called reviews, product reviews, audits, and walk-through; in some application areas, these different terms have narrow and specific meanings.

Results from Scope Verification

1- Formal Acceptance

Documentation that the client or sponsor has accepted the product of the project or phase must be prepared and distributed. Such acceptance may be conditional, especially at the end of a phase.

SCOPE CHANGE CONTROL

Scope change control is concerned with:
(a) influencing the factors which create scope changes to ensure that changes are beneficial,
(b) determining that a scope change has occurred, and
(c) managing the actual changes when and if they occur.

Scope change control must be thoroughly integrated with the other control processes (time control, cost control, quality control, and others as discussed in Chapter 4).

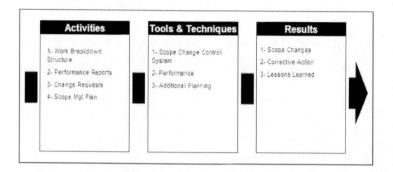

Activities	Tools & Techniques	Results
1- Work Breakdown Structure	1- Scope Change Control System	1- Scope Changes
2- Performance Reports	2- Performance	2- Corrective Action
3- Change Requests	3- Additional Planning	3- Lessons Learned
4- Scope Mgt Plan		

Activities to Scope Change Control

1- Work Breakdown Structure (WBS)

The Work Breakdown Structure (WBS) is described in Chapter 5. It defines the project's scope baseline.

2- Performance Reports

Performance reports discussed in Chapter 10 provide information on scope performance such as which interim products have been completed and which have not. Performance reports may also alert the project team to issues which may cause problems in the future.

3- Change Requests

Change requests may occur in many forms, oral or written, direct or indirect, externally or internally initiated, and legally mandated or optional. Changes may require expanding the scope or may allow shrinking it. Most change requests are the result of:

- An external event (e.g., a change in a government regulation).
- An error or omission in defining the scope of the product (e.g., failure to include a required feature in the design of a telecommunications system).
- An error or omission in defining the scope of the project (e.g., using a bill of materials instead of a work breakdown structure).
- A value-adding change (e.g., an environmental remediation project is able to reduce costs by taking advantage of technology that was not available when the scope was originally defined).

4- Scope Management Plan
The scope management plan is described in Chapter 5.

Tools and Techniques for Scope Change Control

1- Scope Change Control System
A scope change control system defines the procedures by which the project scope may be changed. It includes the paperwork, tracking systems, and approval levels necessary for authorizing changes. The scope change control system should be integrated with the overall change control system described in Chapter 4 and, in particular, with any system or systems in place to control *product* scope. When the project is done under contract, the scope change control system must also comply with all relevant contractual provisions.

2- Performance Measurement

Performance measurement techniques, described in Chapter 10, help to assess the magnitude of any variations which do occur. An important part of scope change control is to determine what is causing the variance and to decide if the variance requires corrective action.

3- Additional Planning

Few projects run exactly according to plan. Prospective scope changes may require modifications to the WBS or analysis of alternative approaches.

Results from Scope Change Control

1- Scope Changes

A scope change is any modification to the agreed upon project scope as defined by the approved WBS. Scope changes often require adjustments to cost, time, quality, or other project objectives. Scope changes are fed back through the planning process, technical and planning documents are updated as needed, and stakeholders are notified as appropriate.

2- Corrective Action

Corrective action is anything done to bring expected future project performance into line with the project plan.

3- Lessons Learned

The causes of variances, the reasoning behind the corrective action chosen, and other types of lessons learned from scope change control should be documented so that this information becomes part of the historical database for both this project and other projects of the performing organization.

CHAPTER 6

PROJECT TIME MANAGEMENT

Project Time Management includes the processes required to ensure timely completion of the project. Figure 6-1 provides an overview of the following major processes:

- Activity Definition - identifying the specific activities that must be performed to produce the various project deliverables.
- Activity Sequencing - identifying and documenting interactivity dependencies.
- Activity Duration Estimating - estimating the number of work periods which will be needed to complete individual activities.
- Schedule Development - analyzing activity sequences, activity durations, and resource requirements to create the project schedule.
- Schedule Control - controlling changes to the project schedule.

These processes interact with each other and with the processes in the other areas as well. Each process may involve effort from one or more individuals or groups of individuals based on the needs of the project. Each process generally occurs at least once in every project phase.

Figure 6-1. Project Time Management Overview

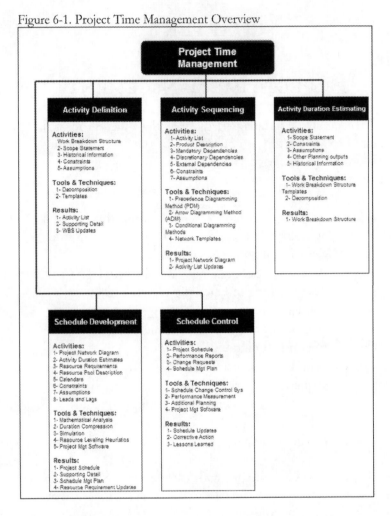

Although the processes are presented here as discrete elements with well-defined interfaces, in practice they may overlap and interact in ways not detailed here. Process interactions are discussed in detail in Chapter 3.

On some projects, especially smaller ones, activity sequencing, activity duration estimating, and schedule development are so tightly linked that they are viewed as a single process (e.g., they may be performed by a single individual over a relatively short period of time). They are presented here as distinct processes because the tools and techniques for each are different.

At present, there is no consensus within the project management profession about the relationship between *activities* and *tasks:*

- In many application areas, activities are seen as being composed of tasks. This is the most common usage and also the preferred usage.
- In others, tasks are seen as being composed of activities.

However, the important consideration is not the term used, but whether or not the work to be done is described accurately and understood by those "who must do the work.

ACTIVITY DEFINITION

Activity definition involves identifying and documenting the specific activities that must be performed in order to produce the deliverables and sub-deliverables identified in the Work Breakdown Structure (WBS). Implicit in this process is the need to define the activities such that the project objectives will be met.

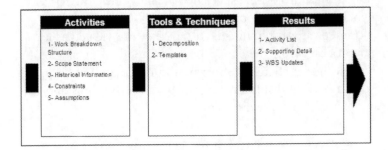

Activities to Activity Definition

1- Work Breakdown Structure (WBS)

The work breakdown structure is the primary input to activity definition (see Chapter 5 for a more detailed discussion of the WBS).

2- Scope Statement

The project justification and the project objectives contained in the scope statement must be considered explicitly during activity definition (see Chapter 5 for a more detailed discussion of the scope statement).

3- Historical Information

Historical information (what activities were actually required on previous, similar projects) should be considered in defining project activities.

4- Constraints

Constraints are factors that will limit the project management team's options.

5- Assumptions

Assumptions are factors that, for planning purposes, will be considered to be true, real, or certain. Assumptions generally involve a degree of risk and will normally be an output of risk identification (described in Chapter 11).

Tools and Techniques for Activity Definition

1- Decomposition
Decomposition involves subdividing project elements into smaller, more manageable components in order to provide better management control. Decomposition is described in more detail in Chapter 5. The major difference between decomposition here and in scope definition is that the final outputs here are described as activities (action steps) rather than as deliverables (tangible items). In some application areas, the WBS and the activity list are developed concurrently.

2- Templates
An activity list (described in Chapter 6), or a portion of an activity list from a previous project, is often usable as a template for a new project. In addition, the activity list for a WBS element from the current project may be usable as a template for other, similar WBS elements.

Results from Activity Definition

1- Activity List
The activity list must include all activities which will be performed on the project. It should be organized as an extension to the WBS to help ensure that it is complete and that it does not include any activities which are not required as part of the project scope. As with the WBS, the activity list should include descriptions of each activity

to ensure that the project team members will understand how the work is to be done.

2- Supporting Detail

Supporting detail for the activity list should be documented and organized as needed to facilitate its use by other project management processes. Supporting detail should always include documentation of all identified assumptions and constraints. The amount of additional detail varies by application area.

3- Work Breakdown Structure Updates

In using the WBS to identify which activities are needed, the project team may identify missing deliverables or may determine that the deliverable descriptions need to be clarified or corrected. Any such updates must be reflected in the WBS and related documentation such as cost estimates.

These updates are often called *refinements* and are most likely when the project involves new or unproven technology.

ACTIVITY SEQUENCING

Activity sequencing involves identifying and documenting inter activity dependencies. Activities must be sequenced accurately in order to support later development of a realistic and achievable schedule. Sequencing can be performed with the aid of a computer (e.g., by using project management software) or with manual techniques. Manual techniques are often more effective on smaller projects and in the early phases of larger ones when little detail is available. Manual and automated techniques may also be used in combination.

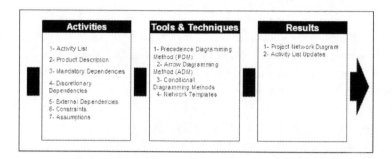

Activities to Activity Sequencing

Activity List
The activity list is described in Chapter 6.

1- Product Description
The product description is discussed in Chapter 5. Product characteristics often affect activity sequencing (e.g., the physical layout of a plant to be constructed, subsystem interfaces on a software project). While these effects are often apparent in the activity list, the product description should generally be reviewed to ensure accuracy.

2- Mandatory Dependencies
Mandatory dependencies are those which are inherent in the nature of the work being done. They often involve physical limitations (on a construction project it is impossible to erect the superstructure until after the foundation has been built; on an electronics project, a

prototype must be built before it can be tested). Mandatory dependencies are also called *hard logic*.

3- Discretionary Dependencies

Discretionary dependencies are those which are defined by the project management team. They should be used with care (and fully documented) since they may limit later scheduling options. Discretionary dependencies are usually defined based on knowledge of:

- "Best practices" within a particular application area.
- Some unusual aspect of the project where a specific sequence is desired even though there are other acceptable sequences. Discretionary dependencies may also be called *preferred logic, preferential logic,* or *soft logic*.

4- External Dependencies

External dependencies are those that involve a relationship between project activities and non-project activities. For example, the testing activity in a software project may be dependent on delivery of hardware from an external source, or environmental hearings may need to be held before site preparation can begin on a construction project.

5- Constraints

Constraints are described in Chapter 6.

6- Assumptions

Assumptions are described in Chapter 6.

Tools and Techniques for Activity Sequencing

1- Precedence Diagramming Method (PDM)

This is a method of constructing a project network diagram using nodes to represent the activities and connecting them with arrows that show the dependencies (see also Chapter 6). Figure 6-2 shows a simple project network diagram drawn using Precedence Diagramming Method (PDM).

Figure 6-2. Network Logic Drawn Using the Precedence Diagramming Method

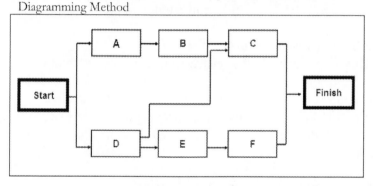

This technique is also called *Activity-on-Node* (AON) and is the method used by most project management software packages. Precedence Diagramming Method (PDM) can be done manually or on a computer. It includes four types of dependencies or precedence relationships:

- Finish-to-start-the "from" activity must finish before the "to" activity can start.

- Finish-to-finish-the "from" activity must finish before the "to" activity can finish.
- Start-to-start-the "from" activity must start before the "to" activity can start.
- Start-to-finish-the "from" activity must start before the "to" activity can finish.

In PDM, finish-to-start is the most commonly used type of logical relationship. Start-to-finish relationships are rarely used, and then typically only by professional scheduling engineers. Using start-to-start, finish-to-finish, or start-to-finish relationships with project management software can produce unexpected results since these types of relationships have not been consistently implemented.

2- Arrow Diagramming Method (ADM)

This is a method of constructing a project network diagram using arrows to represent the activities and connecting them at nodes to show the dependencies (see Chapter 6). Figure 6-3 shows a simple project network diagram drawn using Arrow Diagramming Method (ADM).

Figure 6-3. Network Logic Diagram Drawn Using the Arrow Diagramming Method

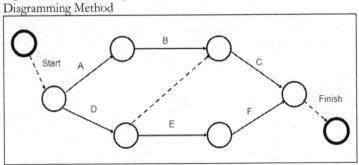

This technique is also called *Activity-on-Arrow* (AOA) and, although less prevalent than Precedence Diagramming Method (PDM), is still the technique of choice in some application areas. Arrow Diagramming Method (ADM) uses only finish-to-start dependencies and may require the use of dummy activities to define all logical relationships correctly. ADM can be done manually or on a computer.

3- Conditional Diagramming Methods

Diagramming techniques such as Graphical Evaluation and Review Technique (GERT) and System Dynamics models allow for non-sequential activities such as loops (e.g., a test that must be repeated more than once) or conditional branches (e.g., a design update that is only needed if the inspection detects errors). Neither Precedence Diagramming Method (PDM) nor Arrow Diagramming Method (ADM) allow loops or conditional branches.

4- Network Templates

Standardized networks can be used to expedite the preparation of project network diagrams. They can include an entire project or only a portion of it. Portions of a network are often referred to as *subnets* or *fragnets*. Subnets are especially useful where a project includes several identical or nearly identical features such as floors on a high-rise office building, clinical trials on a pharmaceutical research project, or program modules on a software project.

Results from Activity Sequencing

1- Project Network Diagram

A project network diagram is a schematic display of the project's activities and the logical relationships (dependencies) among them. Figures 6-2 and 6-3 (previous pages) illustrate two different approaches to drawing a project network diagram.

A project network diagram may be produced manually or on a computer. It may include full project details or have one or more summary activities (hammocks). The diagram should be accompanied by a summary narrative that describes the basic sequencing approach. Any unusual sequences should be fully described.

The project network diagram is often incorrectly called a *PERT chart* (Program Evaluation and Review Technique). A PERT chart is a specific type of project network diagram that is seldom used today.

2- Activity List Updates

In much the same manner that the activity definition process may generate updates to the WBS, preparation of the project network diagram may reveal instances where an activity must be divided or otherwise redefined in order to diagram the correct logical relationships.

ACTIVITY DURATION ESTIMATING

Activity duration estimating involves assessing the number of work periods likely to be needed to complete each identified activity. The person or group on the project team who is most familiar with the nature of a specific activity should make, or at least approve, the estimate. Estimating the number of work periods required to complete an activity will often require consideration of elapsed time as well. For example, if "concrete curing" will require four days of elapsed time, it may require from two to four work periods based on (a) which day of the week it begins on and (b) whether or not weekend days are treated as work periods. Most computerized scheduling software will handle this problem automatically.

Overall project duration may also be estimated using the tools and techniques presented here, but it is more properly calculated as the output of schedule development (described in Chapter 6).

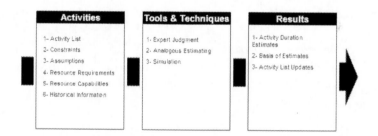

Activities for Project Duration Estimating

1- Activity List
The activity list is described in Chapter 6.

1- Constraints
Constraints are described in Chapter 6.

2- Assumptions
Assumptions are described in Chapter 6.

3- Resource Requirements

Resource requirements are described in Chapter 7. The duration of most activities will be significantly influenced by the resources assigned to them. For example, two people working together may be able to complete a design activity in half the time it takes either of them individually, while a person working half-time on an activity will generally take at least twice as much time as the same person working full-time.

4- Resource Capabilities

The duration of most activities will be significantly influenced by the capabilities of the humans and material resources assigned to them. For example, if both are assigned full-time, a senior staff member can generally be expected to complete a given activity in less time than a junior staff member.

5- Historical Information

Historical information on the likely durations of many categories of activities is often available from one or more of the following sources:

- Project files - one or more of the organizations involved in the project may maintain records of previous project results that are detailed enough to aid in developing duration estimates. In some application areas, individual team members may maintain such records.
- Commercial duration estimating databases - historical information is often available commercially. These databases tend to be especially useful when activity durations are not driven by the actual work content (e.g., how long does it take concrete to cure; how long does a

government agency usually take to respond to certain types of requests).

- Project team knowledge - the individual members of the project team may remember previous actual or estimates. While such recollections may be useful, they are generally far less reliable than documented results.

Tools and Techniques for Activity Duration Estimating

1- Expert Judgment

Expert judgment is described in Chapter 5 Durations are often difficult to estimate because of the number of factors which can influence them (e.g., resource levels, resource productivity). Expert judgment guided by historical information should be used whenever possible. If such expertise is not available, the estimates are inherently uncertain and risky (see Chapter 11, Project Risk Management).

2- Analogous Estimating

Analogous estimating, also called *top-down estimating,* means using the actual duration of a previous, similar activity as the basis for estimating the duration of a future activity. It is frequently used to estimate project duration when there is a limited amount of detailed information about the project (e.g., in the early phases). Analogous estimating is a form of expert judgment (described in Chapter 6). Analogous estimating is most reliable when (a) the previous activities are similar in fact and not *just* in appearance, and (b) the individuals preparing the estimates have the needed expertise.

3- Simulation

Simulation involves calculating multiple durations with different sets of assumptions. The most common is Monte Carlo Analysis in which a distribution of probable results is defined for each activity and used to calculate a distribution of probable results for the total project (see Chapter 11, Schedule Simulation).

Results from Activity Duration Estimating

1- Activity Duration Estimates

Activity duration estimates are quantitative assessments of the likely number of work periods that will be required to complete an activity. Activity duration estimates should always include some indication of the range of possible results. For example:

- 2 weeks ± 2 days to indicate that the activity will take at least 8 days and no more than 12.
- 15 percent probability of exceeding 3 weeks to indicate a high probability - 85 percent that the activity will take 3 weeks or less. Chapter 11 on Project Risk Management includes a more detailed discussion of estimating uncertainty.

2- Basis of Estimates

Assumptions made in developing the estimates must be documented.

3- Activity List Updates

Activity list updates are described in Chapter 6.

SCHEDULE DEVELOPMENT

Schedule development means determining start and finish dates for project activities. If the start and finish dates are not realistic, the project is unlikely to be finished as scheduled. The schedule development process must often be iterated (along with the processes that provide inputs, especially duration estimating and cost estimating) prior to determination of the project schedule.

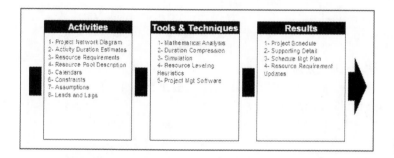

Activities to Schedule Development

1- Project Network Diagram
The project network diagram is described in Chapter 6.

2- Activity duration estimates
Activity duration estimates are described in Chapter 6.

3- Resource Requirements
Resource requirements are described in chapter 6.

4- Resource Pool Description
Knowledge of what resources will be available at what

times and in what patterns is necessary for schedule development. For example, shared resources can be especially difficult to schedule since their availability may be highly variable.

The amount of detail and the level of specificity in the resource pool description will vary. For example, for preliminary schedule development of a consulting project one need only know that two consultants will be available in a particular timeframe.

The final schedule for the same project, however, must identify which specific consultants will be available.

5- Calendars

Project and resource calendars identify periods when work is allowed. *Project calendars* affect all resources (e.g., some projects will work only during normal business hours while others will work a full three shifts). *Resource calendars* affect a specific resource or category of resources (e.g., a project team member may be on vacation or in a training program; a labor contract may limit certain workers to certain days of the week).

6- Constraints

Constraints are described in Chapter 6. There are two major categories of constraints that must be considered during schedule development:

- Imposed dates. Completion of certain deliverables by a specified date may be *required* by the project sponsor, the project customer, or other external factors (e.g., a market window on a technology project; a court-mandated completion date on an environmental remediation project).

- Key events or major milestones. Completion of certain deliverables by a specified date may be *requested* by the project sponsor, the project customer, or other stakeholders. Once scheduled, these dates become expected and often may be moved only with great difficulty.

7- Assumptions

Assumptions are described in Chapter 6.

8- Leads and Lags

Any of the dependencies may require specification of a lead or a lag in order to accurately define the relationship (e.g., there might be a two-week delay between ordering a piece of equipment and installing or using it).

Tools and Techniques for Schedule Development

1- Mathematical Analysis

Mathematical analysis involves calculating theoretical early and late start and finish dates for all project activities without regard for any resource pool limitations. The resulting dates are not the schedule, but rather indicate the time periods within which the activity *should* be scheduled given resource limits and other known constraints. The most widely known mathematical analysis techniques are:

- Critical Path Method (CPM) - calculates a single, deterministic early and late start and finish date for each activity based on specified, sequential network logic and a single duration estimate. The focus of CPM is on calculating *float* in order to determine which activities have the least scheduling flexibility. The underlying CPM algorithms are often used in other types of mathematical analysis.

- Graphical Evaluation and Review Technique (GERT) - allows for probabilistic treatment of both network logic and activity duration estimates (i.e., some activities may not be performed at all, some may be performed only in part, and others may be performed more than once).

- Program Evaluation and Review Technique (PERT) - uses sequential network logic and a weighted average duration estimate to calculate project duration. Although there are surface differences, PERT differs from CPM primarily in that it uses the distribution's mean (expected value) instead of the most likely estimate originally used in CPM (see Figure 6-4). PERT itself is seldom used today although PERT-like estimates are often used in CPM calculations.

Figure 6-4. PERT Duration Calculation

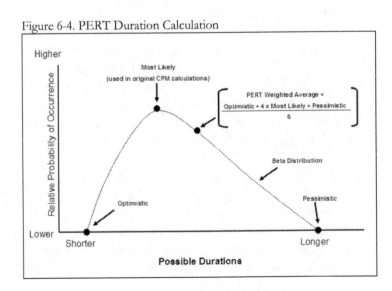

2- Duration Compression

Duration compression is a special case of mathematical analysis that looks for ways to shorten the project schedule without changing the project scope (e.g., to meet imposed dates or other schedule objectives). Duration compression includes techniques such as:

- Crashing - in which cost and schedule trade-offs are analyzed to determine how to obtain the greatest amount of compression for the least incremental cost. Crashing does not always produce a viable alternative and often results in increased cost.

- Fast tracking - doing activities in parallel that would normally be done in sequence (e.g., starting to write code on a software project before the design is complete, or starting to build the foundation for a petroleum processing plant before the 25 percent of engineering point is reached). Fast tracking often results in rework and usually increases risk.

3- Simulation

Simulation is described in Chapter 6.

4- Resource Leveling Heuristics

Mathematical analysis often produces a preliminary schedule that requires more resources during certain time periods than are available, or requires changes in resource levels that are not manageable. Heuristics such as "allocate scarce resources to critical path activities first" can be applied to develop a schedule that reflects such constraints. Resource leveling often results in a project duration that is longer than the preliminary schedule. This technique is sometimes called the "Resource-based

Method," especially when implemented with computerized optimization.

Resource constrained scheduling is a special case of resource leveling where the heuristic involved is a limitation on the quantity of resources available.

5- Project Management Software
Project management software is widely used to assist with schedule development. These products automate the calculations of mathematical analysis and resource leveling and thus allow for rapid consideration of many schedule alternatives. They are also widely used to print or display the outputs of schedule development.

Results from Schedule Development

1- Project Schedule
The project schedule includes at least planned start and expected finish dates for each detail activity. (Note: the project schedule remains preliminary until resource assignments have been confirmed. This would usually happen no later than the completion of Project Plan Development, Chapter 4).

The project schedule may be presented in summary form (the "master schedule") or in detail. Although it can be presented in tabular form, it is more often presented graphically using one or more of the following formats:

- Project network diagrams with date information added (see Figure 6-5). These charts usually show both the project logic and the project's critical path activities (see Chapter 6 for more information on project network diagrams).

Figure 6-5. Project Network Diagram with Scheduled Dates

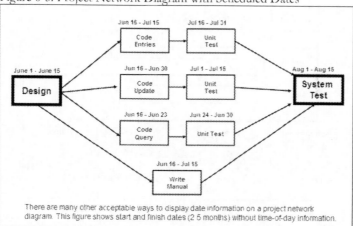

There are many other acceptable ways to display date information on a project network diagram. This figure shows start and finish dates (2 5 months) without time-of-day information.

- Bar charts, also called Gantt charts (see Figure 6-6), show activity start and end dates as well as expected durations, but do not usually show dependencies.

Figure 6-6. Bar (Gantt) Chart

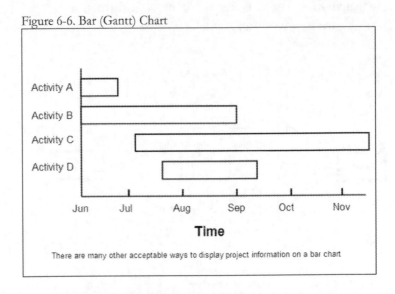

• They are relatively easy to read and are frequently used in management presentations.
• Milestone charts (see Figure 6-7), similar to bar charts, but identifying the scheduled start or completion of major deliverables and key external interfaces.

Figure 6-7. Milestone Chart

Event	Jan	Feb	Mar	Apr	May	Jun	Jul	Aug
Subcontracts Signed			△ ▼					
Specifications Finalized				△ ▽				
Design Reviewed					△			
Subsystem Tested						△		
First Unit Delivered							△	
Production Plan Completed								△

Data Date (at Mar/Apr boundary)

There are many other acceptable ways to display project information on a milestone chart

- Time-scaled network diagrams (see Figure 6-8) are a blend of project network diagrams and bar charts in that they show project logic, activity durations, and schedule information.

Figure 6-8. Time-Scaled Network Diagram

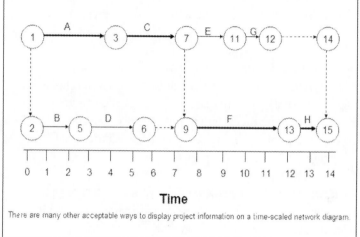

2- Supporting Detail

Supporting detail for the project schedule includes at least documentation of all identified assumptions and constraints. The amount of additional detail varies by application area. For example:

- On a construction project, it will most likely include such items as resource histograms, cash flow projections, and order and delivery schedules.
- On an electronics project, it will most likely include resource histograms only.

Information frequently supplied as supporting detail includes, but is not limited to:

- Resource requirements by time period, often in the form of a resource histogram.
- Alternative schedules (e.g., best case or worst case, resource leveled or not, with or without imposed dates).
- Schedule reserves or schedule risk assessments (see Chapter 11).

3- Schedule Management Plan

A schedule management plan defines how changes to the schedule will be managed. It may be formal or informal, highly detailed or broadly framed based on the needs of the project. It is a subsidiary element of the overall project plan (see Chapter 4).

4- Resource Requirement Updates

Resource leveling and activity list updates may have a significant effect on preliminary estimates of resource requirements.

SCHEDULE CONTROL

Schedule control is concerned with (a) influencing the factors which create schedule changes to ensure that changes are beneficial, (b) determining that the schedule has changed, and (c) managing the actual changes when and as they occur. Schedule control must be thoroughly integrated with the other control processes as described in Chapter 4, Overall Change Control.

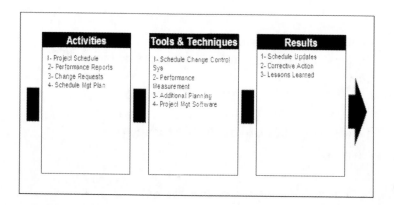

Activities to Schedule Control

1- Project Schedule

The project schedule is described in Chapter 6. The approved project schedule, called the schedule baseline, is a component of the overall project plan described in Chapter 4. It provides the basis for measuring and reporting schedule performance.

2- Performance Reports

Performance reports, discussed in Chapter 10, provide information on schedule performance such as which planned dates have been met and which have not. Performance reports may also alert the project team to issues which may cause problems in the future.

3- Change Requests

Change requests may occur in many forms - oral or written, direct or indirect, externally or internally initiated, and legally mandated or optional. Changes may require extending the schedule or may allow accelerating it.

4- Schedule Management Plan

The schedule management plan is described in Chapter 6.

Tools and Techniques for Schedule Control

1- Schedule Change Control System

A schedule change control system defines the procedures by which the project schedule may be changed. It includes the paperwork, tracking systems, and approval levels necessary for authorizing changes. Schedule change control should be integrated with the overall change control system described in Chapter 4.

2- Performance Measurement

Performance measurement techniques such as those described in Chapter 10 help to assess the magnitude of any variations which do occur. An important part of schedule control is to decide if the schedule variation requires corrective action. For example, a major delay on a non-critical activity may have little effect on the overall project while a much shorter delay on a critical or near-critical activity may require immediate action.

3- Additional Planning

Few projects run exactly according to plan. Prospective changes may require new or revised activity duration estimates, modified activity sequences, or analysis of alternative schedules.

4- *Project Management Software*

Project management software is described in Chapter 6. The ability of project management software to track planned dates versus actual dates and to forecast the effects of schedule changes, real or potential, makes it a useful tool for schedule control.

Results from Schedule Control

1- *Schedule Updates*

A schedule update is any modification to the schedule information which is used to manage the project. Appropriate stakeholders must be notified as needed. Schedule updates may or may not require adjustments to other aspects of the overall project plan. *Revisions* are a special category of schedule updates. Revisions are changes to the scheduled start and finish dates in the approved project schedule. These dates are generally revised only in response to scope changes. In some cases, schedule delays may be so severe that "re-base-lining" is needed in order to provide realistic data to measure performance.

2- *Corrective Action*

Corrective action is anything done to bring expected future schedule performance into line with the project plan. Corrective action in the area of time management often involves expediting: special actions taken to ensure completion of an activity on time or with the least possible delay.

3- *Lessons Learned*

The causes of variances, the reasoning behind the corrective action chosen, and other types of lessons

learned from schedule control should be documented so
that they become part of the historical database for both
this project and other projects of the performing
organization.

CHAPTER 7

PROJECT COST MANAGEMENT

Project Cost Management includes the processes required to ensure that the project is completed within the approved budget. Figure 7-1 provides an overview of the following major processes:

- Resource Planning - determining what resources (people, equipment, materials) and what quantities of each should be used to perform project activities.
- Cost Estimating - developing an approximation (estimate) of the costs of the resources needed to complete project activities.
- Cost Budgeting - allocating the overall cost estimate to individual work items.
- Cost Control - controlling changes to the project budget.

These processes interact with each other and with the processes in the other areas as well. Each process may involve effort from one or more individuals or groups of individuals based on the needs of the project. Each process generally occurs at least once in every project phase.

Although the processes are presented here as discrete elements with well-defined interfaces, in practice they may overlap and interact in ways not detailed here. Process interactions are discussed in detail in Chapter 3.
Figure 7-1 .Provides an overview of the Project Cost Mgt

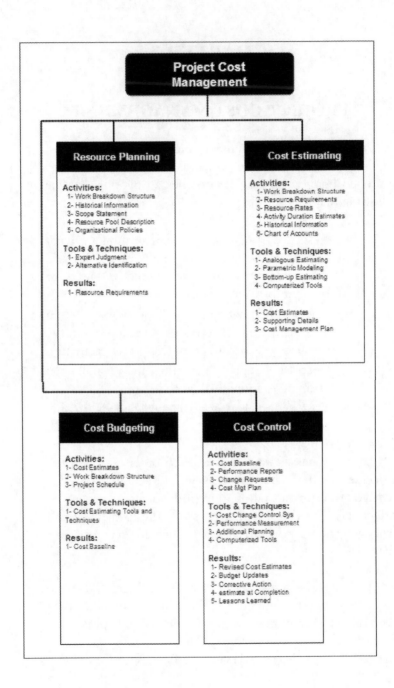

Project Cost Management

Resource Planning

Activities:
1- Work Breakdown Structure
2- Historical Information
3- Scope Statement
4- Resource Pool Description
5- Organizational Policies

Tools & Techniques:
1- Expert Judgment
2- Alternative Identification

Results:
1- Resource Requirements

Cost Estimating

Activities:
1- Work Breakdown Structure
2- Resource Requirements
3- Resource Rates
4- Activity Duration Estimates
5- Historical Information
6- Chart of Accounts

Tools & Techniques:
1- Analogous Estimating
2- Parametric Modeling
3- Bottom-up Estimating
4- Computerized Tools

Results:
1- Cost Estimates
2- Supporting Details
3- Cost Management Plan

Cost Budgeting

Activities:
1- Cost Estimates
2- Work Breakdown Structure
3- Project Schedule

Tools & Techniques:
1- Cost Estimating Tools and Techniques

Results:
1- Cost Baseline

Cost Control

Activities:
1- Cost Baseline
2- Performance Reports
3- Change Requests
4- Cost Mgt Plan

Tools & Techniques:
1- Cost Change Control Sys
2- Performance Measurement
3- Additional Planning
4- Computerized Tools

Results:
1- Revised Cost Estimates
2- Budget Updates
3- Corrective Action
4- estimate at Completion
5- Lessons Learned

Project cost management is primarily concerned with the cost of the resources needed to complete project activities. However, project cost management should also consider the effect of project decisions on the cost of using the project product. For example, limiting the number of design reviews may reduce the cost of the project at the expense of an increase in the customer's operating costs. This broader view of project cost management is often called *life-cycle costing*.

In many application areas predicting and analyzing the prospective financial performance of the project product is done outside the project. In others (e.g., capital facilities projects), project cost management also includes this work. When such predictions and analysis are included, project cost management will include additional processes and numerous general management techniques such as return on investment, discounted cash flow, payback analysis, and others.

Project cost management should consider the information needs of the project stakeholder's different stakeholders may measure project costs in different ways and at different times. For example, the cost of a procurement item may be measured when committed, ordered, delivered, incurred, or recorded for accounting purposes.

When project costs are used as a component of a reward and recognition system (reward and recognition systems are discussed in Chapter 9), controllable and uncontrollable costs should be estimated and budgeted separately to ensure that rewards reflect actual performance.

On some projects, especially smaller ones, resource planning, cost estimating, and cost budgeting are so tightly linked that they are viewed as a single process (e.g., they may be performed by a single individual over a relatively short period of time). They are presented here as distinct processes because the tools and techniques for each are different.

RESOURCE PLANNING

Resource planning involves determining what physical resources (people, equipment, materials) and what quantities of each should be used to perform project activities.

It must be closely coordinated with cost estimating (described in Chapter 7). For example:

- A construction project team will need to be familiar with local building codes. Such knowledge is often readily available at virtually no cost by using local labor. However, if the local labor pool lacks experience with unusual or specialized construction techniques, the additional cost for a consultant might be the most effective way to secure knowledge of the local building code.

- An automotive design team should be familiar with the latest in automated assembly techniques. The requisite knowledge might be obtained by hiring a consultant, by sending a designer to a seminar on robotics, or by including someone from manufacturing as a member of the team.

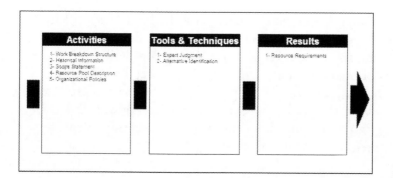

Activities to Resource Planning

1- *Work Breakdown Structure (WBS)*

The Work Breakdown Structure (WBS) (described in Chapter 5) identifies the project elements that will need resources and thus is the primary input to resource planning. Any relevant outputs from other planning processes should be provided through the WBS to ensure proper control.

2- *Historical Information*

Historical information regarding what types of resources were required for similar work on previous projects should be used if available.

3- *Scope Statement*

The scope statement (described in Chapter 5) contains the project justification and the project objectives, both of which should be considered explicitly during resource planning.

4- *Resource Pool Description*

Knowledge of what resources (people, equipment, and material) are potentially available is necessary for resource planning; the amount of detail and the level of specificity of the resource pool description will vary. For example, during the early phases of an engineering design project, the pool may include "junior and senior engineers" in large numbers. During later phases of the same project, however, the pool may be limited to those individuals who are knowledgeable about the project as a result of having worked on the earlier phases.

5- Organizational Policies

The policies of the performing organization regarding staffing and the rental or purchase of supplies and equipment must be considered during resource planning.

Tools and Techniques for Resource Planning

1- Expert Judgment

Expert judgment will often be required to assess the inputs to this process. Such expertise may be provided by any group or individual with specialized knowledge or training and is available from many sources including:

- Other units within the performing organization.
- Consultants.
- Professional and technical associations.
- Industry groups.

2- Alternatives Identification

Alternatives identification is discussed in Chapter 5.

Results from Resource Planning

1- Resource Requirements

The output of the resource planning process is a description of what types of resources are required and in what quantities for each element of the work breakdown structure. These resources will be obtained either through staff acquisition (described in Chapter 9) or procurement (described in Chapter 12).

COST ESTIMATING

Cost estimating involves developing an approximation (estimate) of the costs of the resources needed to complete project activities. When a project is performed under contract, care should be taken to distinguish cost estimating from pricing. Cost estimating involves developing an assessment of the likely quantitative result - how much will it cost the performing organization to provide the product or service involved. Pricing is a business decision - how much will the performing organization charge for the product or service - that uses the cost estimate as but one consideration of many.

Cost estimating includes identifying and considering various costing alternatives. For example, in most application areas, additional work during a design phase is widely held to have the potential for reducing the cost of the production phase. The cost estimating process must consider whether the cost of the additional design work will offset the expected savings.

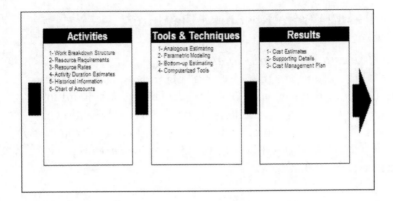

Activities to Cost Estimating

1- Work Breakdown Structure (WBS)

The WBS is described in Chapter 5. It will be used to organize the cost estimates and to ensure that all identified work has been estimated.

2- Resource Requirements

Resource requirements are described in Chapter 7.

3- Resource Rates

The individual or group preparing the estimates must know the unit rates (e.g., staff cost per hour, bulk material cost per cubic yard) for each resource in order to calculate project costs. If actual rates are not known, the rates themselves may have to be estimated.

4- Activity Duration Estimates

Activity duration estimates (described in Chapter 6) will affect cost estimates on any project where the project budget includes an allowance for the cost of financing (i.e., interest charges).

5- Historical Information

Information on the cost of many categories of resources is often available from one or more of the following sources:

- Project files - one or more of the organizations involved in the project may maintain records of previous project results that are detailed enough to aid in developing cost estimates. In some application areas, individual team members may maintain such records.
- Commercial cost estimating databases - historical information is often available commercially.
- Project team knowledge - the individual members of the project team may remember previous actual or estimates. While such recollections may be useful, they are generally far less reliable than documented results.

Chart of Accounts

A chart of accounts describes the coding structure used by the performing organization to report financial information in its general ledger. Project cost estimates must be assigned to the correct accounting, category.

Tools and Techniques for Cost Estimating

1- Analogous Estimating

Analogous estimating, also called *top-down estimating*, means using the actual cost of a previous, similar project as the basis for estimating the cost of the current project. It is frequently used to estimate total project costs when there is a limited amount of detailed information about the project (e.g., in the early phases). Analogous estimating is a form of expert judgment (described in Chapter 7). Analogous estimating is generally less costly than other techniques, but it is also generally less accurate. It is most reliable when (a) the previous projects are similar in fact and not just in appearance, and (b) the individuals or groups preparing the estimates have the needed expertise.

2- Parametric Modeling

Parametric modeling involves using project characteristics (parameters) in a mathematical model to predict project costs. Models may be simple (residential home construction will cost a certain amount per square foot of living space) or complex (one model of software development costs uses 13 separate adjustment factors each of which has 5-7 points on it). Both the cost and accuracy of parametric models varies widely. They are most likely to be reliable when (a) the historical information used to develop the model was accurate, (b) the parameters used in the model are readily quantifiable, and (c) the model is scalable (i.e., it works as well for a very large project as for a very small one).

3- Bottom-up Estimating

This technique involves estimating the cost of individual work items, then summarizing or rolling-up the individual estimates to get a project total. The cost and accuracy of bottom-up estimating is driven by the size' of the individual work items: smaller work items increase both cost and accuracy. The project management team must weigh the additional accuracy against the additional cost.

4- Computerized Tools

Computerized tools such as project management software and spreadsheets are widely used to assist with cost estimating. Such products can simplify the use of the tools described above and thereby facilitate rapid consideration of many costing alternatives.

Results from Cost Estimating

1- Cost Estimates

Cost estimates are quantitative assessments of the likely costs of the resources required to complete project activities. They may be presented in summary or in detail. Costs must be estimated for all resources that will be charged to the project. This includes, but is not limited to, labor, materials, supplies, and special categories such as an inflation allowance or cost reserve. Cost estimates are generally expressed in units of currency (dollars, francs, yen, etc.) in order to facilitate comparisons both within and across projects. Other units such as staff hours or staff days may be used, unless doing so will misstate project costs (e.g., by failing to differentiate among resources with very different costs). In some cases, estimates will have to be provided using multiple units of measure in order to facilitate appropriate management control.

Cost estimates may benefit from being refined during the course of the project to reflect the additional detail available. In some application areas, there are guidelines for when such refinements should be made and what degree of accuracy is expected. For example, AACE (Association for the Advancement of Cost Engineering) has identified a progression of five types of estimates of construction costs during engineering: order of magnitude, conceptual, preliminary, definitive, and control.

2- *Supporting Detail*

Supporting detail for the cost estimates should include:

- A description of the scope of work estimated. This is often provided by a reference to the WBS.
- Documentation of the basis for the estimate, i.e., how it was developed.
- Documentation of any assumptions made.
- An indication of the range of possible results, for example, $10,000 \pm $1,000 to indicate that the item is expected to cost between $9,000 and $11,000. The amount and type of additional detail varies by application area. Retaining even rough notes may prove valuable by providing a better understanding of how the estimate was developed.

3- *Cost Management Plan*

The cost management plan describes how cost variances will be managed (e.g., different responses to major problems than to minor ones). A cost management plan may be formal or informal, highly detailed or broadly framed based on the needs of the project stakeholders. It is a subsidiary element of the overall project plan (discussed in Chapter 4).

COST BUDGETING

Cost budgeting involves allocating the overall cost estimates to individual work items in order to establish a cost baseline for measuring project performance.

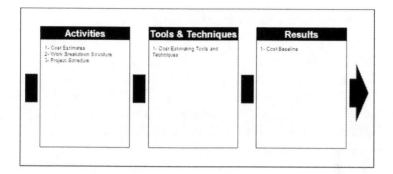

Activities to Cost Budgeting

1- Cost Estimates
Cost estimates are described in Chapter 7.

2- Work Breakdown Structure (WBS)
The work breakdown structure (described in Chapter 5) identifies the project elements that costs will be allocated to.

3- Project Schedule
The project schedule (described in Chapter 6) includes planned start and expected finish dates for the project elements that costs will be allocated to. This information is needed in order to assign costs to the time period when the cost will be incurred.

Tools and Techniques for Cost Budgeting

1- Cost Estimating Tools and Techniques
The tools and techniques described in Chapter 7 for developing project cost estimates are used to develop budgets for work items as well.

Results from Cost Budgeting

2- Cost Baseline

The cost baseline is a time-phased budget that will be used to measure and monitor cost performance on the project. It is developed by summing estimated costs by period and is usually displayed in the form of an S-curve, as illustrated in Figure 7-2.

Figure 7-2. Illustrative Cost Baseline Display

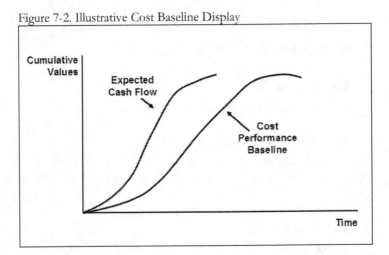

Many projects, especially larger ones, may have multiple cost baselines to measure different aspects of cost performance. For example, a spending plan or cash flow forecast is a cost baseline for measuring disbursements.

COST CONTROL

Cost control is concerned with (a) influencing the factors which create changes to the cost baseline to ensure that changes are beneficial, (b) determining that the cost

baseline has changed, and (c) managing the actual changes
when and as they occur. Cost control includes:

- Monitoring cost performance to detect variances
  from plan.
- Ensuring that all appropriate changes are recorded
  accurately in the cost baseline.
- Preventing incorrect, inappropriate, or
  unauthorized changes from being included in the
  cost baseline.
- Informing appropriate stakeholders of authorized
  changes.

Cost control includes searching out the "whys" of
both positive and negative variances. It must be
thoroughly integrated with the other control processes
(scope change control, schedule control, quality control,
and others as discussed in Chapter 4). For example,
inappropriate responses to cost variances can cause quality
or schedule problems or produce an unacceptable level of
risk later in the project.

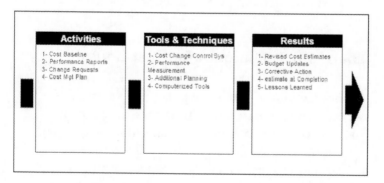

Activities to Cost Control

1- Cost Baseline
The cost baseline is described in Chapter 7.

2- Performance Reports
Performance reports (discussed in Chapter 10) provide information on cost performance such as which budgets have been met and which have not. Performance reports may also alert the project team to issues which may cause problems in the future.

3- Change Requests
Change requests may occur in many forms, oral or written, direct or indirect, externally or internally initiated, and legally mandated or optional. Changes may require increasing the budget or may allow decreasing it.

4- Cost management Plan
The cost management plan is described in Chapter 7.

Tools and Techniques for Cost Control

1- Cost Change Control System
A cost change control system defines the procedures by which the cost baseline may be changed. It includes the paperwork, tracking systems, and approval levels necessary for authorizing changes. The cost change control system should be integrated with the overall change control system discussed in Chapter 4.

2- Performance Measurement

Performance measurement techniques, described in Chapter 10, help to assess the magnitude of any variations which do occur. Earned value analysis, described in Chapter 10, is especially useful for cost control. An important part of cost control is to determine what is causing the variance and to decide if the variance requires corrective action.

3- Additional Planning

Few projects run exactly according to plan. Prospective changes may require new or revised cost estimates or analysis of alternative approaches.

4- Computerized Tools

Computerized tools such as project management software and spreadsheets are often used to track planned costs vs. actual costs, and to forecast the effects of cost changes.

Results from Cost Control

1- Revised Cost Estimates

Revised cost estimates are modifications to the cost information used to manage the project. Appropriate stakeholders must be notified as needed. Revised cost estimates mayor may not require adjustments to other aspects of the overall project plan.

2- Budget Updates

Budget updates are a special category of revised cost estimates. Budget updates are changes to an approved cost baseline. These numbers are generally revised only in response to scope changes. In some cases, cost variances may be so severe that "re-base-lining" is needed in order to provide a realistic measure of performance.

3- Corrective Action

Corrective action is anything done to bring expected future project performance into line with the project plan.

4- Estimate at Completion

An Estimate At Completion (EAC) is a forecast of total project costs based on project performance. The most common forecasting techniques are some variation of:

- EAC = Actual to date plus the remaining project budget modified by a performance factor, often the cost performance index (described in Chapter 10). This approach is most often used when current variances are seen as typical of future variances.
- EAC = Actual to date plus a new estimate for all remaining work. This approach is most often used when past performance shows that the original estimating assumptions were fundamentally flawed, or that they are no longer relevant due to a change in conditions.
- EAC = Actual to date plus remaining budget. This approach is most often used when current variances are seen as atypical and the project management team's expectation is that similar variances will not occur in the future. Each of the above approaches may be the correct approach for any given work item.

5- Lessons Learned

The causes of variances, the reasoning behind the corrective action chosen, and other types of lessons learned from cost control should be documented so that they become part of the historical database for both this project and other projects of the performing organization.

CHAPTER 8

PROJECT QUALITY MANAGEMENT

Project Quality Management includes the processes required to ensure that the project will satisfy the needs for which it was undertaken. According to International Organization for Standardization (1993) "all activities of the overall management function that determine the quality policy, objectives, and responsibilities and implements them by means such as quality planning, quality control, quality assurance, and quality improvement, within the quality system". Figure 8-1 provides an overview of the following major project quality management processes:

- Quality Planning - identifying which quality standards are relevant to the project and determining how to satisfy them.
- Quality Assurance - evaluating overall project performance on a regular basis to provide confidence that the project will satisfy the relevant quality standards.
- Quality Control - monitoring specific project results to determine if they comply with relevant quality standards and identifying ways to eliminate causes of unsatisfactory performance.

These processes interact with each other and with the processes in the other areas as well. Each process may involve effort from one or more individuals or groups of

individuals based on the needs of the project. Each
process generally occurs at least once in every project
phase.

Figure 8-1. Project Quality Management Overview

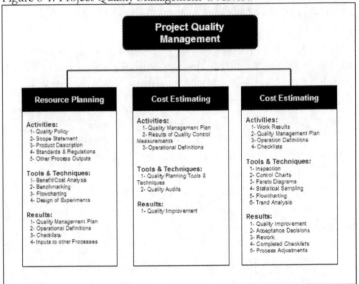

Although the processes are presented here as discrete
elements with well-defined interfaces, in practice they may
overlap and interact in ways not detailed here. Process
interactions are discussed in detail in Chapter 3, Project
Management Processes. The basic approach to quality
management described in this section is intended to be
compatible with that of the International Organization for
Standardization (ISO).

This generalized approach should also be compatible
with (a) proprietary approaches to quality management
such as those recommended by Deming (1986), Juran
(1988 & 1992), Crosby (1996 & 1979), and others, and (b)

non-proprietary approaches such as Total Quality Management (TQM), Continuous Improvement, and others.

Project quality management must address both the management of the project and the product of the project. Failure to meet quality requirements in either dimension can have serious negative consequences for any or all of the project stakeholders. For example:

- Meeting customer requirements by overworking the project team may produce negative consequences in the form of increased employee turnover.

- Meeting project schedule objectives by rushing planned quality inspections may produce negative consequences when errors go undetected.

According to International Organization for Standardization (1993) Quality is "the totality of characteristics of an entity that bear on its ability to satisfy stated or implied needs". A critical aspect of quality management in the project context is the necessity to turn implied needs into stated needs through project scope management, which is described in Chapter 5.

The project management team must be careful not to confuse *quality* with *grade*. According to International Organization for Standardization (1993) Grade is "a category or rank given to entities having the same functional use but different requirements for quality". Low quality is always a problem; low grade may not be. For example, a software product may be of high quality (no obvious bugs, readable manual) and low grade (a limited number of features), or of low quality (many bugs, poorly organized user documentation) and high grade (numerous features).

Determining and delivering the required levels of both quality and grade are the responsibilities of the project manager and the project management team. The project management team should also be aware that modern quality management complements modern project management. For example, both disciplines recognize the importance of:

- Customer satisfaction - understanding, managing, and influencing needs so that customer expectations are met or exceeded. This requires a combination of *conformance to specifications* (the project must produce what it said it would produce) and *fitness for use* (the product or service produced must satisfy real needs).
- Prevention over inspection - the cost of avoiding mistakes is always much less than the cost of correcting them.
- Management responsibility - success requires the *participation* of all members of the team, but it remains the *responsibility* of management to provide the resources needed to succeed.
- Processes within phases - the repeated plan-do-check-act cycle described by Deming and others is highly similar to the combination of phases and processes (discussed in Chapter 3).

In addition, quality improvement initiatives undertaken by the performing organization (e.g., Total Quality Management (TQM), Continuous Improvement, and others) can improve the quality of the project management as well as the quality of the project product.

However, there is an important difference that the project management team must be acutely aware of - the temporary nature of the project means that investments in product quality improvement, especially defect prevention and appraisal, must often be borne by the performing organization since the project may not last long enough to reap the rewards.

QUALITY PLANNING

Quality planning involves identifying which quality standards are relevant to the project and determining how to satisfy them. It is one of the key facilitating processes during project planning (see Chapter 3, Planning Processes) and should be performed regularly and in parallel with the other project planning processes. For example, the desired management quality may require cost or schedule adjustments, or the desired product quality may require a detailed risk analysis of an identified problem. Prior to development of the International Organization for Standardization (ISO) Series, the activities described here as *quality planning* were widely discussed as part of *quality assurance*.

The quality planning techniques discussed here are those used most frequently on projects. There are many others that may be useful on certain projects or in some application areas.

The project team should also be aware of one of the fundamental tenets of modern quality management - quality is planned in, not inspected in.

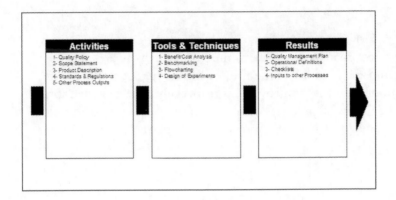

Activities to Quality Planning

1- Quality Policy

According to International Organization for Standardization (1993) Quality policy is "the overall intentions and direction of an organization with regard to quality, as formally expressed by top management". The quality policy of the performing organization can often be adopted "as is" for use by the project. However, if the performing organization lacks a formal quality policy, or if the project involves multiple performing organizations (as with a joint venture), the project management team will need to develop a quality policy for the project. Regardless of the origin of the quality policy, the project management team is responsible for ensuring that the project stakeholders are fully aware of it (e.g., through appropriate information distribution, as described in Chapter 10).

2- Scope Statement

The scope statement (described in Chapter 5) is a key input to quality planning since it documents major project deliverables as well as the project objectives which serve to define important stakeholder requirements.

3- Product Description

Although elements of the product description (described in Chapter 5) may be embodied in the scope statement, the product description will often contain details of technical issues and other concerns that may affect quality planning.

4- Standards and Regulations

The project management team must consider any application-area-specific standards or regulations that may affect the project. Chapter 2 discusses standards and regulations.

5- Other Process Outputs

In addition to the scope statement and product description, processes in other areas may produce outputs that should be considered as part of quality planning. For example, procurement planning (described in Chapter 12) may identify contractor quality requirements that should be reflected in the overall quality management plan.

Tools and Techniques for Quality Planning

1- Benefit/Cost Analysis

The quality planning process must consider benefit/cost trade-offs, as described in Chapter 5. The primary benefit of meeting quality requirements is less rework, which means higher productivity, lower costs, and increased stakeholder satisfaction. The primary cost of meeting quality requirements is the expense associated with project quality management activities. It is axiomatic of the quality management discipline that the benefits our weigh the costs.

2- Benchmarking

Benchmarking involves comparing actual or planned project practices to those of other projects in order to generate ideas for improvement and to provide a standard by which to measure performance. The other projects may be within the performing organization or outside of it, and may be within the same application area or in another.

3- Flowcharting

A flowchart is any diagram which shows how various elements of a system relate. Flowcharting techniques commonly used in quality management include:

Cause-and-effect diagrams (figure 8-2), also called *Ishikawa diagrams* or *fishbone diagrams,* which illustrate how various causes and sub causes relate to create potential problems or effects.

Figure 8-2. Cause-and-effect Diagram

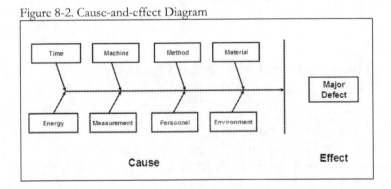

System or *process flowcharts,* which show how various elements of a system interrelate.

Figure 8-3 is an example of a process flowchart for design reviews.

Figure 8-3 is an example of a generic cause-and-effect diagram.

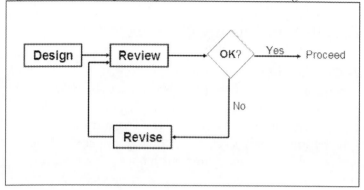

Flowcharting can help the project team anticipate what and where quality problems might occur and thus can help to develop approaches to dealing with them.

4- Design of Experiments

Design of experiments is an analytical technique which helps identify which variables have the most influence on the overall outcome. The technique is applied most frequently to product of the project issues (e.g., automotive designers might wish to determine which combination of suspension and tires will produce the most desirable ride characteristics at a reasonable cost).

However, it can also be applied to project management issues such as cost and schedule trade-offs. For example, senior engineers will cost more than junior engineers, but can also be expected to complete the assigned work in less time. An appropriately designed "experiment" (in this case, computing project costs and durations for various combinations of senior and junior engineers) will often allow determination of an optimal solution from a relatively limited number of cases.

Results from Quality Planning

1- Quality Management Plan
The quality management plan should describe how the project management team will implement its quality policy. According to International Organization for Standardization (1993) the project quality system is "the organizational structure, responsibilities, procedures, processes, and resources needed to implement quality management". The quality management plan provides input to the overall project plan (described in Chapter 4, Project Plan Development) and must address quality control, quality assurance, and quality improvement for the project. The quality management plan may be formal or informal, highly detailed, or broadly framed, based on the needs of the project.

2- Operational Definitions
An operational definition describes, in very specific terms, what something is, and how it is measured by the quality control process. For example, it is not enough to say that meeting the planned schedule dates is a measure of management quality; the project management team must also indicate whether every activity must start on time, or only finish on time; whether individual activities will be measured or only certain deliverables, and if so, which ones. Operational definitions are also called *metrics* in some application areas.

3- Checklists

A checklist is a structured tool, usually industry or activity-specific, used to verify that a set of required steps has been performed. Checklists may be simple or complex. They are usually phrased as imperatives ("Do this!") or interrogatories ("Have you done this?"). Many organizations have standardized checklists available to ensure consistency in frequently performed activities. In some application areas, checklists are also available from professional associations or commercial service providers.

4- Inputs to Other Processes

The quality planning process may identify a need for further activity in another area.

QUALITY ASSURANCE

Quality assurance is all the planned and systematic activities implemented within the quality system to provide confidence that the project will satisfy the relevant quality standards. It should be performed throughout the project. Prior to development of the ISO Series, the activities described under *quality planning* were widely included as part of *quality assurance*.

Quality assurance is often provided by a Quality Assurance Department or similarly titled organizational unit, but it does not have to be. Assurance may be provided to the project management team and to the management of the performing organization (internal quality assurance) or it may be provided to the customer and others not actively involved in the work of the project (external quality assurance).

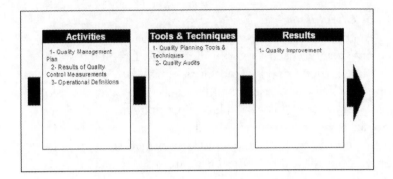

Activities to Quality Assurance

1- Quality Management Plan
The quality management plan is described in Chapter 8.

2- Results of Quality Control Measurements
Quality control measurements are records of quality control testing and measurement in a format for comparison and analysis.

3- Operational Definitions
Operational definitions are described in Chapter 8.

Tools and Techniques for Quality Assurance

1- Quality Planning Tools and Techniques
The quality planning tools and techniques (described in Chapter 8) can be used for quality assurance as well.

2- Quality Audits

A quality audit is a structured review of other quality management activities. The objective of a quality audit is to identify lessons learned that can improve performance of this project or of other projects within the performing organization. Quality audits may be scheduled or random, and they may be carried out by properly trained in-house auditors or by third parties such as quality system registration agencies.

Results from Quality Assurance

1- Quality Improvement

Quality improvement includes taking action to increase the effectiveness and efficiency of the project to provide added benefits to the project stakeholders. In most cases, implementing quality improvements will require preparation of change requests or taking of corrective action and will be handled according to procedures for overall change control, as described in Chapter 4.

QUALITY CONTROL

Quality control involves monitoring specific project results to determine if they comply with relevant quality standards and identifying ways to eliminate causes of unsatisfactory results. It should be performed throughout the project. Project results include both *product* results such as deliverables and *management* results such as cost and schedule performance. Quality control is often performed by a Quality Control Department or similarly titled organizational unit, but it does not have to be.

The project management team should have a working knowledge of statistical quality control, especially sampling and probability, to help them evaluate quality control outputs. Among other subjects, they should know the differences between:

- Prevention (keeping errors out of the process) and inspection (keeping errors out of the hands of the customer).

- Attribute sampling (the result conforms or it does not) and variables sampling (the result is rated on a continuous scale that measures the degree of conformity).

- Special causes (unusual events) and random causes (normal process variation).

- Tolerances (the result is acceptable if it falls within the range specified by the tolerance) and control limits (the process is in control if the result falls within the control limits).

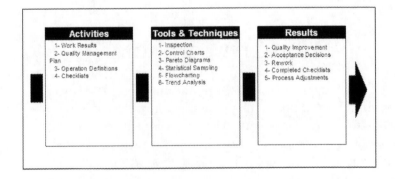

Activities to Quality Control

1- Work Results
Work results (described in Chapter 4) include both *process* results and *product* results. Information about the planned or expected results from the project plan should be available along with information about the actual results.

2- Quality Management Plan
The quality management plan is described in Chapter 8.

3- Operational Definitions
Operational definitions are described in Chapter 8.

4- Checklists
Checklists are described in Chapter 8.

Tools and Techniques for Quality Control

1- Inspection
Inspection includes activities such as measuring, examining, and testing undertaken to determine whether results conform to requirements. Inspections may be conducted at any level (e.g., the results of a single activity may be inspected or the final product of the project may be inspected). Inspections are variously called reviews, product reviews, audits, and walk-through in some application areas; these terms have narrow and specific meanings.

2- *Control Charts*

Control charts are a graphic display of the results, over time, of a process. They are used to determine if the process is "in control" (e.g., are differences in the results created by random variations or are unusual events occurring whose causes must be identified and corrected?). When a process is in control, the process should not be adjusted. The process may be changed in order to provide improvements but it should not be adjusted when it is in control. Control charts may be used to monitor any type of output variable. Although used most frequently to track repetitive activities such as manufactured lots, control charts can also be used to monitor cost and schedule variances, volume and frequency of scope changes, errors in project documents, or other management results to help determine if the "project management process" is in control. Figure 8-4 is a control chart of project schedule performance.

Figure 8-4. Control Chart of Project Schedule Performance

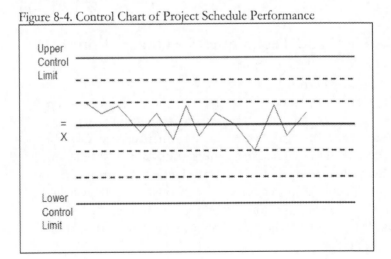

3- Pareto Diagrams

A Pareto diagram is a histogram, ordered by frequency of occurrence that shows how many results were generated by type or category of identified cause (see Figure 8-5). Rank ordering is used to guide corrective action the project team should take action to fix the problems that are causing the greatest number of defects first. Pareto diagrams are conceptually related to Pareto's Law, which holds that a relatively small number of causes will typically produce a large majority of the problems or defects.

Figure 8-5. Pareto Diagram

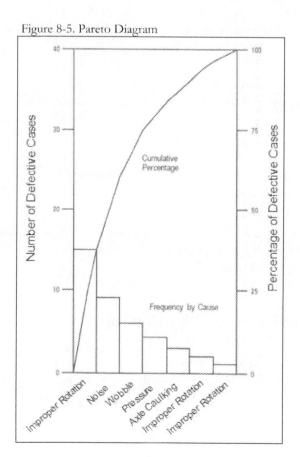

4- Statistical Sampling

Statistical sampling involves choosing part of a population of interest for inspection (e.g., selecting ten engineering drawings at random from a list of 75). Appropriate sampling can often reduce the cost of quality control. There is a substantial body of knowledge on statistical sampling; in some application areas, it is necessary for the project management team to be familiar with a variety of sampling techniques.

5- Flowcharting

Flowcharting is described in Chapter 8. Flowcharting is used in quality control to help analyze how problems occur.

6- Trend Analysis

Trend analysis involves using mathematical techniques to forecast future outcomes based on historical results. Trend analysis is often used to monitor:

- Technical performance - how many errors or defects have been identified, how many remain uncorrected.
- Cost and schedule performance - how many activities per period were completed with significant variances.

Results from Quality Control

1- Quality Improvement

Quality improvement is described in Chapter 8.

2- Acceptance Decisions

The items inspected will be either accepted or rejected. Rejected items may require rework (described in Chapter 8).

3- Rework

Rework is action taken to bring a defective or non-conforming item into compliance with requirements or specifications. Rework, especially unanticipated rework, is a frequent cause of project overruns in most application areas. The project team should make every reasonable effort to minimize rework.

4- Completed Checklists

See Chapter 8. When checklists are used, the completed checklists should become part of the project's records.

5- Process Adjustments

Process adjustments involve immediate corrective or preventive action as a result of quality control measurements. In some cases, the process adjustment may need to be handled according to procedures for overall change control, as described in Chapter 4.

CHAPTER 9

PROJECT HUMAN RESOURCE MANAGEMENT

Project Human Resource Management includes the processes required to make the most effective use of the people involved with the project. It includes all the project Stakeholders, sponsors, customers, individual contributors, and others described in Chapter 2. Figure 9-1 provides an overview of the following major processes:

- Organizational Planning - identifying, documenting, and assigning project roles, responsibilities, and reporting relationships.
- Staff Acquisition - getting the human resources needed assigned to and working on the project.
- Team Development - developing individual and group skills to enhance project performance.

These processes interact with each other and with the processes in the other areas as well. Each process may involve effort from one or more individuals or groups of individuals based on the needs of the project. Although the processes are presented here as discrete elements with well-defined interfaces, in practice they may overlap and interact in ways not detailed here. Process interactions are discussed in detail in Chapter 3, Project Management Processes.

Figure 9-1. Project Human Resource Management Overview

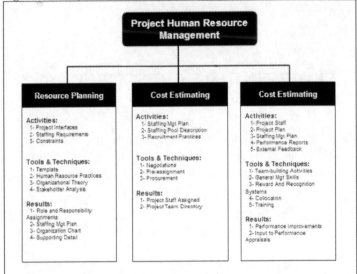

There is a substantial body of literature about dealing with people in an operational, ongoing context. Some of the many topics include:

- Leading, communicating, negotiating, and others (discussed in Chapter 2) Key General Management Skills.
- Delegating, motivating, coaching, mentoring, and other subjects related to dealing with individuals.
- Team building, dealing with conflict, and other subjects related to dealing with groups.
- Performance appraisal, recruitment, retention, labor relations, health and safety regulations, and other subjects related to administering the human resource function.

Most of this material is directly applicable to leading and managing people on projects, and the project manager and project management team should be familiar with it. However, they must also be sensitive as to how this knowledge is applied on the project. For example:

- The temporary nature of projects means that the personal and organizational relationships will generally be both temporary and new. The project management team must take care to select techniques that are appropriate for such transient relationships.

- The nature and number of project stakeholders will often change as the project moves from phase to phase of its life cycle. As a result, techniques that are effective in one phase may not be effective in another. The project management team must take care to use techniques that are appropriate to the current needs of the project.

- Human resource administrative activities are seldom a direct responsibility of the project management team. However, the team must be sufficiently aware of administrative requirements to ensure compliance.

ORGANIZATIONAL PLANNING

Organizational planning involves identifying, documenting, and assigning project roles, responsibilities, and reporting relationships. Roles, responsibilities, and reporting relationships may be assigned to individuals or to groups. The individuals and groups may be part of the organization performing the project or they may be external to it. Internal groups are often associated with a specific functional department such as engineering, marketing, or accounting.

On most projects, the majority of organizational planning is done as part of the earliest project phases. However, the results of this process should be reviewed regularly throughout the project to ensure continued applicability. If the initial organization is no longer effective, it should be revised promptly.

Organizational planning is often tightly linked with communications planning (described in Chapter 10) since the project's organizational structure will have a major effect on the project's communications requirements.

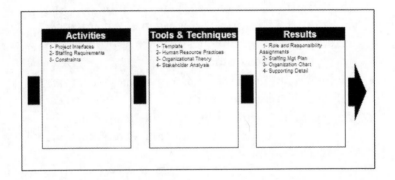

Activities to Organizational Planning

1- Project Interfaces
Project interfaces generally fall into one of three categories:

1. Organizational interfaces - formal and informal reporting relationships among different

organizational units. Organizational interfaces may be highly complex or very simple. For example, developing a complex telecommunications system may require coordinating numerous subcontractors over several years, while fixing a programming error in a system installed at a single site may require little more than notifying the user and the operations staff upon completion.

2. Technical interfaces - formal and informal reporting relationships among different technical disciplines. Technical interfaces occur both within project phases (e.g., the site design developed by the civil engineers must be compatible with the superstructure developed by the structural engineers) and between project phases (e.g., when an automotive design team passes the results of its work along to the retooling team that must create the manufacturing capability for the vehicle).

3. Interpersonal interfaces - formal and informal reporting relationships among different individuals working on the project.

These interfaces often occur simultaneously, as when an architect employed by a design firm explains key design considerations to an unrelated construction contractor's project management team.

2- Staffing Requirements

Staffing requirements define what kinds of skills are required from what kinds of individuals or groups and in what time frames. Staffing requirements are a subset of the overall resource requirements identified during resource planning (described in Chapter 7).

3- Constraints

Constraints are factors that limit the project team's options. A project's organizational options may be constrained in many ways. Common factors that may constrain how the team is organized include, but are not limited to, the following:

- Organizational structure of the performing organization - an organization whose basic structure is a *strong matrix* means a relatively stronger role for the project manager than one whose basic structure is a *weak matrix* (see Chapter 2 for a more detailed discussion of organizational structures).
- Collective bargaining agreements - contractual agreements with unions or other employee groups may require certain roles or reporting relationships (in essence, the employee group is a stakeholder).
- Preferences of the project management team - if members of the project management team have had success with certain structures in the past, they are likely to advocate similar structures in the future.
- Expected staff assignments - how the project is organized is often influenced by the skills and capabilities of specific individuals.

Tools and Techniques for Organizational Planning

1- Templates
Although each project is unique, most projects will resemble another project to some extent. Using the role and responsibility definitions or reporting relationships of a similar project can help expedite the process of organizational planning.

2- Human Resource Practices
Many organizations have a variety of policies, guidelines, and procedures that can help the project management team with various aspects of organizational planning. For example, an organization that views managers as "coaches" is likely to have documentation on how the role of "coach" is to be performed.

3- Organizational Theory
There is a substantial body of literature describing how organizations can and should be structured. Although only a small subset of this body of literature is specifically targeted at project organizations, the project management team should be generally familiar with the subject of organizational theory so as to be better able to respond to project requirements.

4- Stakeholder Analysis
The needs of the various stakeholders should be analyzed to ensure that their needs will be met. Chapter 10 discusses stakeholder analysis in more detail.

Results from Organizational Planning

1- Role and Responsibility Assignments

Project roles (who does what) and responsibilities (who decides what) must be assigned to the appropriate project stakeholders. Roles and responsibilities may vary over time. Most roles and responsibilities will be assigned to stakeholders who are actively involved in the work of the project, such as the project manager, other members of the project management team, and the individual contributors.

The roles and responsibilities of the project manager are generally critical on most projects but vary significantly by application area. Project roles and responsibilities should be closely linked to the project scope definition. A Responsibility Assignment Matrix (RAM), (see Figure 9-2) is often used for this purpose. On larger projects, RAMs may be developed at various levels. For example, a high-level RAM may define which group or unit is responsible for each element of the work breakdown structure while lower-level RAMs are used within the group to assign roles and responsibilities for specific activities to particular individuals.

Figure 9-2. Responsibility Assignment Matrix.

PHASE \ PERSON	A	B	C	D	E	F	...
Requirements	S	R	A	P	P		
Functional	S		A	P		P	
Design	S		R	A	I		P
Development		R	S	A		P	P
Testing			S	P	I	A	P

P=Participant A=Accountable R=Review Required
I=Input Required S=Sign-off Required

2- Staffing Management Plan

The staffing management plan describes when and how human resources will be brought plan may be formal or informal, highly detailed or broadly framed, based on the needs of the project. It is a subsidiary element of the overall project plan (see Chapter 4, Project Plan Development). The staffing management plan often includes resource histograms, as illustrated in Figure 9-3.

Figure 9-3. Illustrative Resource Histogram

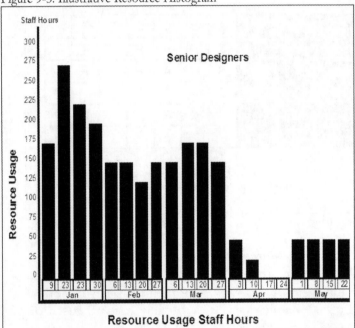

Particular attention should be paid to how project team members (individuals or groups) will be released when they are no longer needed on the project. Appropriate reassignment procedures may:

- Reduce costs by reducing or eliminating the tendency to "make work" to fill the time between this assignment and the next.
- Improve morale by reducing or eliminating uncertainty about future employment opportunities.

3- Organization Chart

An organization chart is any graphic display of project reporting relationships. It may be formal or informal, highly detailed or broadly framed, based on the needs of the project. For example, the organization chart for a three to four person internal service project is unlikely to have the rigor and detail of the organization chart for a 3,000-person nuclear power plant outage. An Organizational Breakdown Structure (OBS) is a specific type of organization chart that shows which organizational units are responsible for which work items.

4- Supporting Detail

Supporting detail for organizational planning varies by application area and project size. Information frequently supplied as supporting detail includes, but is not limited to:

- Organizational impact - what alternatives are precluded by organizing in this manner.
- Job descriptions - written outlines by job title of the skills, responsibilities, knowledge, authority, physical environment, and other characteristics involved in performing a given job. Also called *position descriptions.*
- Training needs - if the staff to be assigned is not expected to have the skills needed by the project, those skills will need to be developed as part of the project.

STAFF ACQUISITION

Staff acquisition involves getting the human resources needed (individuals or groups) assigned to and working on the project. In most environments, the "best" resources may not be available, and the project management team must take care to ensure that the resources which are available will meet project requirements.

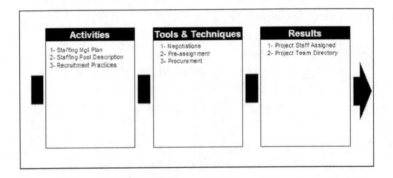

Activities to Staff Acquisition

1- Staffing Management Plan
The staffing management plan is described in Chapter 9. It includes the project's staffing requirements as described in Chapter 9.

2- Staffing Pool Description
When the project management team is able to influence or direct staff assignments, it must consider the characteristics of the potentially available staff. Considerations include, but are not limited to:

- Previous experience - have the individuals or groups done similar or related work before? Have they done it well?
- Personal interests - are the individuals or groups interested in working on this project?
- Personal characteristics - are the individuals or groups likely to work well together as a team?
- Availability - will the most desirable individuals or groups be available in the necessary time frames?

3- Recruitment Practices

One or more of the organizations involved in the project may have policies, guidelines, or procedures governing staff assignments. When they exist, such practices act as a constraint on the staff acquisition process.

Tools and Techniques for Staff Acquisition

1- Negotiations

Staff assignments must be negotiated on most projects. For example, the project management team may need to negotiate with:

- Responsible functional managers to ensure that the project receives appropriately skilled staff in the necessary time frame.
- Other project management teams within the performing organization to assign scarce or specialized resources appropriately.

The team's influencing skills (see Chapter 2, Influencing the Organization) play an important role in negotiating staff assignments as do the politics of the organizations involved. For example, a functional manager may be rewarded based on staff utilization. This creates an incentive for the manager to assign available staff who may not meet all of the project's requirements.

2- Pre-assignment

In some cases, staff may be pre-assigned to the project. This is often the case when (a) the project is the result of a competitive proposal and specific staff was promised as part of the proposal, or (b) the project is an internal service project and staff assignments were defined within the project charter.

3- Procurement

Project procurement management (described in Chapter 12) can be used to obtain the services of specific individuals or groups of individuals to perform project activities. Procurement is required when the performing organization lacks the in-house staff needed to complete the project (e.g., as a result of a conscious decision not to hire such individuals as full-time employees, as a result of having all appropriately skilled staff previously committed to other projects, or as a result of other circumstances).

Results from Staff Acquisition

1- Project Staff Assigned

The project is staffed when appropriate people have been reliably assigned to work on it. Staff may be assigned full-time, part-time, or variably, based on the needs of the project.

2- Project Team Directory

A project team directory lists all the project team members and other key stakeholders. The directory may be formal or informal, highly detailed or broadly framed, based on the needs of the project.

TEAM DEVELOPMENT

Team development includes both enhancing the ability of stakeholders to contribute as individuals as well as enhancing the ability of the team to function as a team. Individual development (managerial and technical) is the foundation necessary to develop the team. Development as a team is critical to the project's ability to meet its objectives.

Team development on a project is often complicated when individual team members are accountable to both a functional manager and to the project manager (see Chapter 2 for a discussion of matrix organizational structures). Effective management of this dual reporting relationship is often a critical success factor for the project and is generally the responsibility of the project manager. Although team development is positioned in Chapter 3 as one of the executing processes, team development occurs throughout the project.

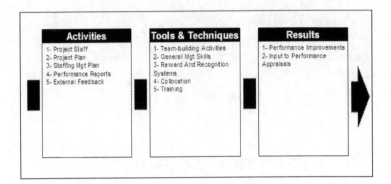

Activities to Team Development

1- Project Staff
Project staffing is described in Chapter 9. The staff assignments implicitly define the individual skills and team skills available to build upon.

2- Project Plan
The project plan is described in Chapter 4. The project plan describes the technical context within which the team operates.

3- Staffing Management Plan
The staffing management plan is described in Chapter 9.

4- Performance Reports
Performance reports (described in Chapter 10) provide feedback to the project team about performance against the project plan.

5- External Feedback

The project team must periodically measure itself against the performance expectations of those outside the project.

Tools and Techniques for Team Development

1- Team-building Activities

Team-building activities include management and individual actions taken specifically and primarily to improve team performance. Many actions, such as involving non-management-level team members in the planning process, or establishing ground rules for surfacing and dealing with conflict, may enhance team performance as a secondary effect. Team-building activities can vary from a five-minute agenda item in a regular status review meeting to an extended, off-site, professionally facilitated experience designed to improve interpersonal relationships among key stakeholders. There is a substantial body of literature on team building. The project management team should be generally familiar with a variety of team-building activities.

2- General Management Skills

General management skills (discussed in Chapter 2) are of particular importance to team development.

3- Reward and Recognition Systems

Reward and recognition systems are formal management actions which promote or reinforce desired behavior. To be effective, such systems must make the link between performance and reward clear, explicit, and achievable. For example, a project manager who is to be rewarded for meeting the project's cost objective should have an appropriate level of control over staffing and procurement decisions. Projects must often have their own reward and recognition systems since the systems of the performing organization may not be appropriate. For example, the willingness to work overtime in order to meet an aggressive schedule objective *should* be rewarded or recognized; needing to work overtime as the result of poor planning *should not* be. Reward and recognition systems must also consider cultural differences. For example, developing an appropriate team reward mechanism in a culture that prizes individualism may be very difficult.

4- Collocation

Collocation involves placing all, or almost all, of the most active project team members in the same physical location to enhance their ability to perform as a team. Collocation is widely used on larger projects and can also be effective for smaller projects (e.g., with a "war room" where the team congregates or leaves in process work items).

5- Training

Training includes all activities designed to enhance the skills, knowledge, and capabilities of the project team. Some authors distinguish among training, education, and development, but the distinctions are neither consistent nor widely accepted.

Training may be formal (e.g., classroom training, computer-based training) or informal (e.g., feedback from other team members). There is a substantial body of literature on how to provide training to adults. If the project team members lack necessary management or technical skills, such skills must be developed as part of the project, or steps must be taken to re-staff the project appropriately. Direct and indirect costs for training are generally paid by the performing organization.

Results from Team Development

1- Performance Improvements
The primary output of team development is improved project performance. Improvements can come from many sources and can affect many areas of project performance, for example:

- Improvements in individual skills may allow a specific person to perform their assigned activities more effectively.

- Improvements in team behaviors (e.g., surfacing and dealing with conflict) may allow project team members to devote a greater percentage of their effort to technical activities.

- Improvements in either individual skills or team capabilities may facilitate identifying and developing better ways of doing project work.

2- Input to Performance Appraisals
Project staff should generally provide input to the performance appraisals of any project staff members that they interact with in a significant way.

CHAPTER 10

PROJECT COMMUNICATIONS MANAGEMENT

Project Communications Management includes the processes required to ensure timely and appropriate generation, collection, dissemination, storage, and ultimate disposition of project information. It provides the critical links among people, ideas, and information that are necessary for success. Everyone involved in the project must be prepared to send and receive communications in the project "language" and must understand how the communications they are involved in as individuals affect the project as a whole. Figure 10-1 provides an overview of the following major processes:

- Communications Planning - determining the information and communications needs of the stakeholders: who needs what information, when will they need it, and how will it be given to them.

- Information Distribution - making needed information available to project stakeholders in a timely manner.

- Performance Reporting - collecting and disseminating performance information. This includes status reporting, progress measurement, and forecasting.

- Administrative Closure-generating, gathering, and disseminating information to formalize phase or project completion.

Figure 10-1. Project Communications Management Overview

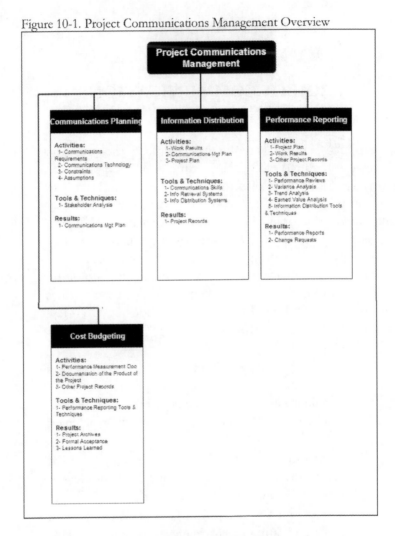

These processes interact with each other and with the processes in the other areas as well. Each process may involve effort from one or more individuals or groups of individuals based on the needs of the project. Each process generally occurs at least once in every project phase.

Although the processes are presented here as discrete elements with well-defined interfaces, in practice they may overlap and interact in ways not detailed here. Process interactions are discussed in detail in Chapter 3.

The general management skill of communicating (discussed in Chapter 2) is related to, but not the same as, project communications management. Communicating is the broader subject and involves a substantial body of knowledge that is not unique to the project context. For example:

- Sender-receiver models - feedback loops, barriers to communications, etc.
- Choice of media - when to communicate in writing versus when to communicate orally, when to write an informal memo versus when to write a formal report, etc.
- Writing style - active versus passive voice, sentence structure, word choice, etc.
- Presentation techniques - body language, design of visual aids, etc.
- Meeting management techniques - preparing an agenda, dealing with conflict, etc.

COMMUNICATIONS PLANNING

Communications planning involves determining the information and communications needs of the stakeholders: who needs what information, when will they need it, and how will it be given to them. While all projects share the need to communicate project information, the informational needs and the methods of distribution vary widely. Identifying the informational needs of the stakeholders and determining a suitable means of meeting those needs is an important factor for project success.

On most projects, the majority of communications planning is done as part of the earliest project phases. However, the results of this process should be reviewed regularly throughout the project and revised as needed to ensure continued applicability.

Communications planning is often tightly linked with organizational planning (described in Chapter 9) since the project's organizational structure will have a major effect on the project's communications requirements.

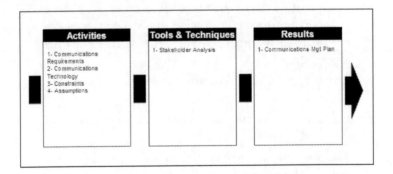

Activities to Communications Planning

1- Communications Requirements

Communications requirements are the sum of the information requirements of the project stakeholders. Requirements are defined by combining the type and format of information required with an analysis of the value of that information. Project resources should be expended only on communicating information which contributes to success or where lack of communication can lead to failure. Information typically required to determine project communications requirements includes:

- Project organization and stakeholder responsibility relationships.
- Disciplines, departments, and specialties involved in the project.
- Logistics of how many individuals will be involved with the project and at which locations.
- External information needs (e.g., communicating with the media).

2- Communications Technology

The technologies or methods used to transfer information back and forth among project elements can vary significantly: from brief conversations to extended meetings, from simple written documents to immediately accessible on-line schedules and databases.

Communications technology factors which may affect the project include:

- The immediacy of the need for information - is project success dependent upon having frequently updated information available on a moment's notice, or would regularly issued written reports suffice?
- The availability of technology - are the systems that are already in place appropriate, or do project needs warrant change?

- The expected project staffing - are the communications systems proposed compatible with the experience and expertise of the project participants, or will extensive training and learning be required?
- The length of the project - is the available technology likely to change before the project is over in a manner that would warrant adopting the newer technology?

3- Constraints

Constraints are factors that will limit the project management team's options. For example, if substantial project resources will be procured, more consideration will need to be given to handling contract information. When a project is performed under contract, there are often specific contractual provisions that affect communications planning.

4- Assumptions

Assumptions are factors that, for planning purposes, will be considered to be true, real, or certain. Assumptions generally involve a degree of risk. They may be identified here or they may be an output of risk identification (described in Chapter 11).

Tools and Techniques for Communications Planning

1- Stakeholder Analysis

The information needs of the various stakeholders should be analyzed to develop a methodical and logical view of their information needs and sources to meet those needs (project stakeholders are discussed in more detail in

Chapters 2 and 5). The analysis should consider methods and technologies suited to the project that will provide the information needed. Care should be taken to avoid wasting resources on unnecessary information or inappropriate technology.

Results from Communications Planning

1- Communications Management Plan
A communications management plan is a document which provides:

- A collection and filing structure which details what methods will be used to gather and store various types of information. Procedures should also cover collecting and disseminating updates and corrections to previously distributed material.
- A distribution structure which details to whom information (status reports, data, schedule, technical documentation, etc.) will flow, and what methods (written reports, meetings, etc.) will be used to distribute various types of information.

This structure must be compatible with the responsibilities and reporting relationships described by the project organization chart.

- A description of the information to be distributed, including format, content, level of detail, and conventions/definitions to be used.
- Production schedules showing when each type of communication will be produced.
- Methods for accessing information between scheduled communications.

- A method for updating and refining the communications management plan as the project progresses and develops.

The communications management plan may be formal or informal, highly detailed or broadly framed, based on the needs of the project. It is a subsidiary element of the overall project plan (described Chapter 4).

INFORMATION DISTRIBUTION

Information distribution involves making needed information available to project stakeholders in a timely manner. It includes implementing the communications management plan as well as responding to unexpected requests for information.

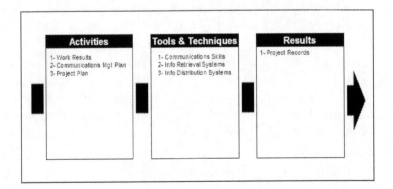

Activities	Tools & Techniques	Results
1- Work Results	1- Communications Skills	1- Project Records
2- Communications Mgt Plan	2- Info Retrieval Systems	
3- Project Plan	3- Info Distribution Systems	

Activities to Information Distribution

1- Work Results
Work results are described in Chapter 4.

2- Communications Management Plan
The communications management plan is described in Chapter 10.

3- Project Plan
The project plan is described in Chapter 4.

Tools and Techniques for Information distribution

1- Communications Skills
Communications skills are used to exchange information. The sender is responsible for making the information clear, unambiguous, and complete so that the receiver can receive it correctly and for confirming that it is properly understood. The receiver is responsible for making sure that the information is received in its entirety and understood correctly. Communicating has many dimensions:

- Written and oral, listening and speaking.
- Internal (within the project) and external (to the customer, the media, the public, etc.).
- Formal (reports, briefings, etc.) and informal (memos, ad hoc conversations, etc.).
- Vertical (up and down the organization) and horizontal (with peers).

2- Information Retrieval Systems

Information can be shared by team members through a variety of methods including manual filing systems, electronic text databases, project management software, and systems which allow access to technical documentation such as engineering drawings.

3- Information Distribution Systems

Project information may be distributed using a variety of methods including project meetings, hard copy document distribution, and shared access to networked electronic databases, fax, electronic mail, voice mail, and video conferencing.

Results from Information Distribution

1- Project Records

Project records may include correspondence, memos, reports, and documents describing the project. This information should, to the extent possible and appropriate, be maintained in an organized fashion. Project team members may often maintain personal records in a project notebook.

PERFORMANCE REPORTING

Performance reporting involves collecting and disseminating performance information in order to provide stakeholders with information about how resources are being used to achieve project objectives. This process includes:

- Status reporting - describing where the project now stands.
- Progress reporting - describing what the project team has accomplished.
- Forecasting - predicting future project status and progress.

Performance reporting should generally provide information on scope, schedule, cost, and quality. Many projects also require information on risk and procurement. Reports may be prepared comprehensively or on an exception basis.

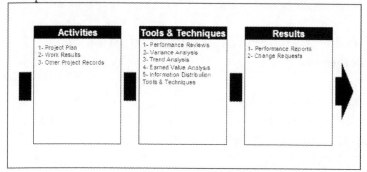

Activities to Performance Reporting

1- Project Plan
The project plan is discussed in Chapter 4. The project plan contains the various baselines that will be used to assess project performance.

2- Work Results
Work results - which deliverables have been fully or partially completed, what costs have been incurred or committed, etc. are an output of project plan execution

(discussed in Chapter 4). Work results should be reported within the framework provided by the communications management plan. Accurate, uniform information on work results is essential to useful performance reporting.

3- Other Project Records
Project records are discussed in Chapter 10. In addition to the project plan and the project's work results, other project documents often contain information pertaining to the project context that should be considered when assessing project performance.

Tools and Techniques for Performance Reporting

1- Performance Reviews
Performance reviews are meetings held to assess project status or progress. Performance reviews are typically used in conjunction with one or more of the performance reporting techniques described below.

2- Variance Analysis
Variance analysis involves comparing actual project results to planned or expected results. Cost and schedule variances are the most frequently analyzed, but variances from plan in the areas of scope, quality, and risk are often of equal or greater importance.

3- Trend Analysis
Trend analysis involves examining project results over time to determine if performance is improving or deteriorating.

4- Earned Value Analysis

Earned value analysis in its various forms is the most commonly used method of performance measurement. It integrates scope, cost, and schedule measures to help the project management team assess project performance.
Earned value involves calculating three key values for each activity:

- The budget, also called the Budgeted Cost of Work Scheduled (BCWS), is that portion of the approved cost estimate planned to be spent on the activity during a given period.
- The actual cost, also called the Actual Cost of Work Performed (ACWP), is the total of direct and indirect costs incurred in accomplishing work on the activity during a given period.
- The earned value, also called the Budgeted Cost of Work Performed (BCWP), is a percentage of the total budget equal to the percentage of the work actually completed.

Many earned value implementations use only a few percentages (e.g., 30 percent, 70 percent, 90 percent, and 100 percent) to simplify data collection. Some earned value implementations use only 0 percent or 100 percent (done or not done) to help ensure objective measurement of performance. These three values are used in combination to provide measures of whether or not work is being accomplished as planned. The most commonly used measures are:

"Cost Variance" (CV = BCWP - ACWP)
"Schedule Variance" (SV = BCWP - BCWS)
"Cost Performance Index" (CPI = BCWP / ACWP)

The cumulative CPI (the sum of all individual BCWIs divided by the sum of all individual ACWPs) is widely used to forecast project cost at completion.

In some application areas, the "Schedule Performance Index" (SPI = BCWP /BCWS) is used to forecast the project completion date.

5- *Information   Distribution   Tools   and Techniques*
Performance reports are distributed using the tools and techniques described in Chapter 10.

Results from Performance Reporting

1- *Performance Reports*
Performance reports organize and summarize the information gathered and present the results of any analysis. Reports should provide the kinds of information and the level of detail required by various stakeholders as documented in the communications management plan. Common formats for performance reports include bar charts (also called Gantt charts), S-curves, histograms, and tables. Figure 10-2 uses S-curves to display cumulative earned value analysis data while Figure 10-3 displays a different set of earned value data in tabular form.

Figure 10-2. Illustrative Graphic Performance Report

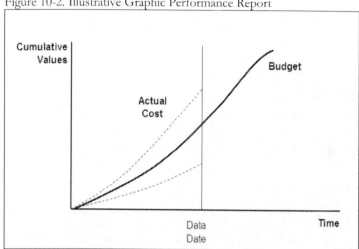

Figure 10-3. Illustrative Tabular Performance Report

WBS Element	Budget($) (BCWS)	Earned Value ($) (BCWP)	Actual Cost($) (ACWP)	CostVariance ($) (BCWP-ACWP)	CostVariance (%) (BCWP÷ACWP)	ScheduleVariance ($) (BCWP-BCWS)	ScheduleVariance (%) (BCWP÷BCWS)
1.0 Pre-pilot planning	63,000	58,000	62,500	-4,500	-7.8	-5,000	-7.9
2.0 Draft checklists	64,000	48,000	46,800	1,200	2.5	-16,000	-25.0
3.0 Curriculum design	23,000	20,000	23,500	-3,500	-17.5	-3,000	-13.0
4.0 Mid-term evaluation	68,000	68,000	72,500	-4,500	-6.6	a	0.0
5.0 Implementation support	12,000	10,000	10,000	0	0.0	-2,000	-16.7
6.0 Manual of practice	7,000	6,200	6,000	200	3.2	-800	-11.4
7.0 Roll-out plan	20,000	13,500	18,100	-4,600	-34.1	-6,500	-32.5
Totals	257,000	223,700	239,400	-15,700	-7.0	-33,300	-13.0

Note: All figures are project-to-date.

2- *Change Requests*

Analysis of project performance often generates a request for a change to some aspect of the project. These change requests are handled as described in the various change control processes (e.g., scope change management, schedule control, etc.).

ADMINISTRATIVE CLOSURE

The project or phase, after either achieving its objectives or being terminated for other reasons, requires closure. Administrative closure consists of verifying and documenting project results to formalize acceptance of the product of the project by the sponsor, client, or customer. It includes collection of project records, ensuring that they reflect final specifications, analysis of project success and effectiveness, and archiving such information for future use.

Administrative closure activities should not be delayed until project completion. Each phase of the project should be properly closed to ensure that important and useful information is not lost.

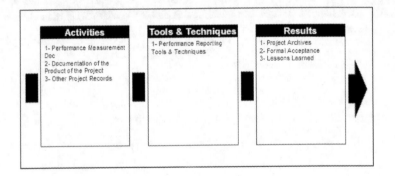

Activities to Administrative Closure

1- Performance Measurement Documentation
All documentation produced to record and analyzes project performance, including the planning documents

which established the framework for performance measurement, must be available for review during administrative closure.

2- Documentation of the Product of the Project

Documents produced to describe the product of the project (plans, specifications, technical documentation, drawings, electronic files, etc. the terminology varies by application area) must also be available for review during administrative closure.

3- Other Project Records

Project records are discussed in Chapter 10.

Tools and Techniques for Administrative Closure

1- Performance Reporting Tools and Techniques

Performance reporting tools and techniques are discussed in Chapter 10.

Results from Administrative Closure
2- Project Archives

A complete set of indexed project records should be prepared for archiving by the appropriate parties. Any project-specific or program-wide historical databases pertinent to the project should be updated. When projects are done under contract or when they involve significant procurement, particular attention must be paid to archiving of financial records.

3- Formal Acceptance

Documentation that the client or sponsor has accepted the product of the project (or phase) should be prepared and distributed.

4- Lessons Learned

Lessons learned are discussed in Chapter 4.

CHAPTER 11

PROJECT RISK MANAGEMENT

Project Risk Management includes the processes concerned with identifying, analyzing, and responding to project risk. It includes maximizing the results of positive events and minimizing the consequences of adverse events. Figure 11-1 provides an overview of the following major processes:

- Risk Identification - determining which risks are likely to affect the project and documenting the characteristics of each.

- Risk Quantification - evaluating risks and risk interactions to assess the range of possible project outcomes.

- Risk Response Development - defining enhancement steps for opportunities and responses to threats.

- Risk Response Control - responding to changes in risk over the course of the project.

These processes interact with each other and with the processes in the other areas as well. Each process may involve effort from one or more individuals or groups of individuals based on the needs of the project. Each process generally occurs at least once in every project phase.

Figure 11-1. Project Risk Management Overview

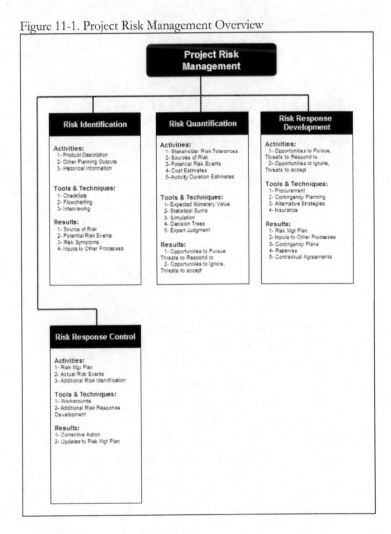

Although the processes are presented here as discrete elements with well defined interfaces, in practice they may overlap and interact in ways not detailed here. Process interactions are discussed in detail in Chapter 3. Different application areas often use different names for the processes described here. For example:

- Risk identification and risk quantification are sometimes treated as a single process, and the combined process may be called risk analysis or risk assessment.
- Risk response development is sometimes called response planning or risk mitigation.
- Risk response development and risk response control are sometimes treated as a single process, and the combined process may be called risk management.

RISK IDENTIFICATION

Risk identification consists of determining which risks are likely to affect the project and documenting the characteristics of each. Risk identification is not a onetime event; it should be performed on a regular basis throughout the project. Risk identification should address both internal and external risks. Internal risks are things that the project team can control or influence, such as staff assignments and cost estimates. External risks are things beyond the control or influence of the project team, such as market shifts or government action.

Strictly speaking, risk involves only the possibility of suffering harm or loss. In the project context, however, risk identification is also concerned with opportunities (positive outcomes) as well as threats (negative outcomes).

Risk identification may be accomplished by identifying causes-and-effects (what could happen and what will ensue) or effects-and-causes (what outcomes are to be avoided or encouraged and how each might occur).

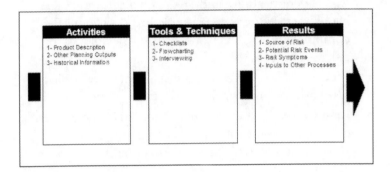

Activities to Risk Identification

1- Product Description
The nature of the product of the project will have a major effect on the risks identified. Products that involve proven technology will, all other things being equal, involve less risk than products which require innovation or invention. Risks associated with the product of the project are often described in terms of their cost and schedule impact. Chapter 5 has additional information about the product Description.

2- Other Planning Outputs
The outputs of the processes in other process areas should be reviewed to identify possible risks. For example:

* Work Breakdown Structure (WBS) - non-traditional approaches to detail deliverables may offer opportunities that were not apparent from

the higher-level deliverables identified in the scope statement.

- Cost estimates and duration estimates - aggressive estimates and estimates developed with a limited amount of information entail more risk.

- Staffing plan - identified team members may have unique skills that would be hard to replace or may have other commitments that make their availability tenuous.

- Procurement management plan - market conditions such as a sluggish local economy may offer opportunities to reduce contract costs.

3- Historical Information

Historical information about what actually happened on previous projects can be especially helpful in identifying potential risks. Information on historical results is often available from the following sources:

- Project files - one or more of the organizations involved in the project may maintain records of previous project results that are detailed enough to aid in risk identification. In some application areas, individual team members may maintain such records.

- Commercial databases - historical information is available commercially in many application areas.

- Project team knowledge - the individual members of the project team may remember previous occurrences or assumptions. While such recollections may be useful, they are generally less reliable than documented results.

Tools and Techniques for Risk Identification

1- Checklists

Checklists are typically organized by source of risk. Sources include the project context (see Chapter 2), other process outputs (see Chapter 11), the product of the project or technology issues, and internal sources such as team member skills (or the lack thereof). Some application areas have widely used classification schemes for sources of risk.

2- Flowcharting

Flowcharting (described in Chapter 8) can help the project team better understand the causes and effects of risks.

3- Interviewing

Risk-oriented interviews with various stakeholders may help identify risks not identified during normal planning activities. Records of pre-project interviews (e.g., those conducted during a feasibility study) may also be available.

Results from Risk Identification

1- Sources of Risk

Sources of risk are categories of possible risk events (e.g., stakeholder actions, unreliable estimates, team turnover) that may affect the project for better or worse. The list of sources should be comprehensive, i.e., it should generally include all identified items regardless of frequency, probability of occurrence, or magnitude of gain or loss. Common sources of risk include:

- Changes in requirements.
- Design errors, omissions, and misunderstandings.
- Poorly defined or understood roles and responsibilities.
- Poor estimates.
- Insufficiently skilled staff.

Descriptions of the sources of risk should generally include estimates of (a) the probability that a risk event from that source will occur, (b) the range of possible outcomes, (c) expected timing, and (d) anticipated frequency of risk events from that source. Both probabilities and outcomes may be specified as continuous functions (an estimated cost between $100,000 and $150,000) or as discrete ones (a patent either will or will not be granted). In addition, estimates of probabilities and outcomes made during early project phases are likely to have a broader range than those made later in the project.

2- Potential Risk Events

Potential risk events are discrete occurrences such as a natural disaster or the departure of a specific team member that may affect the project. Potential risk events should be identified in addition to sources of risk when the probability of occurrence or magnitude of loss is relatively large ("relatively large" will vary by project). While potential risk events are seldom application-area-specific, a list of *common* risk events usually is. For example:

- Development of new technology that will obviate the need for a project is common in electronics and rare in real estate development.
- Losses due to a major storm are common in construction and rare in biotechnology.

Descriptions of potential risk events should generally include estimates of (a) the probability that the risk event will occur, (b) the alternative possible outcomes, (c) expected timing of the event, and (d) anticipated frequency (i.e., can it happen more than once). Both probabilities and outcomes may be specified as continuous functions (an estimated cost between $100,000 and $150,000) or as discrete ones (a patent either will or will not be granted). In addition, estimates of probabilities and outcomes made during early project phases are likely to have a broader range than those made later in the project.

3- Risk Symptoms
Risk symptoms, sometimes called triggers, are indirect manifestations of actual risk events. For example, poor morale may be an early warning signal of an impending schedule delay or cost overruns on early activities may be indicative of poor estimating.

4- Inputs to Other Processes
The risk identification process may identify a need for further activity in another area. For example, the work breakdown structure may not have sufficient detail to allow adequate identification of risks. Risks are often input to the other processes as constraints or assumptions.

RISK QUANTIFICATION

Risk quantification involves evaluating risks and risk interactions to assess the range of possible project outcomes. It is primarily concerned with determining which risk events warrant response. It is complicated by a number of factors including, but not limited to:

- Opportunities and threats can interact in unanticipated ways (e.g., schedule delays may force consideration of a new strategy that reduces overall project duration).

- A single risk event can cause multiple effects, as when late delivery of a key component produces cost overruns, schedule delays, penalty payments, and a lower-quality product.

- Opportunities for one stakeholder (reduced cost) may be threats to another (reduced profits).

- The mathematical techniques used can create a false impression of precision and reliability.

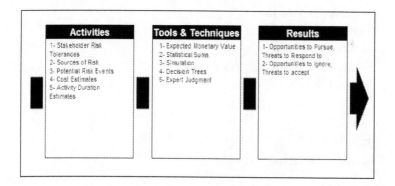

Activities to Risk Quantification

1- Stakeholder Risk Tolerances

Different organizations and different individuals have different tolerances for risk. For example:

- A highly profitable company may be willing to spend $500,000 to write a proposal for a $1 billion contract, while a company operating at break-even is not.

- One organization may perceive an estimate that has a 15 percent probability of overrunning as high risk, while another perceives it as low risk.

Stakeholder risk tolerances provide a screen for both inputs and outputs to risk quantification.

2- Sources of Risk
Sources of risk are described in Chapter 11.

3- Potential Risk Events
Potential risk events are described in Chapter 11.

4- Cost Estimates
Cost estimates are described in Chapter 7.

5- Activity Duration Estimates
Activity duration estimates are described in Chapter 6.

Tools and Techniques for Risk Quantification

1- Expected Monetary Value
Expected monetary value, as a tool for risk quantification, is the product of two numbers:

1. Risk event probability - an estimate of the probability that a given risk event will occur.
2. Risk event value - an estimate of the gain or loss that will be incurred if the risk event does occur.

The risk event value must reflect both tangibles and intangibles. For example, Project A and Project B both identify an equal probability of a tangible loss of $100,000 as an outcome of an aggressively priced proposal. If Project A predicts little or no intangible effect, while Project B predicts that such a loss will put its performing organization out of business, the two risks are not equivalent.

Figure 11-2. Summing Probability Distributions

Activity Name	Low	Most Likely	High	Mean	Sigma	Variance
	a	m	b	$\bar{x}$	σ	σ^2
Triangular Distribution						
Initial Draft						
Gather Information	40	45	80	55.0	8.9	79.2
Write Sections	35	50	100	61.7	13.9	193.1
Review Informally	10	15	30	18.3	4.2	18.1
Inspection						
Inspectors Inspect	18	25	50	31.0	6.9	47.2
Prepare Defects/Issues List	10	20	40	23.3	6.2	38.9
Resolve Defects/Issues	10	25	60	31.7	10.5	109.7
Make Necessary Changes	15	20	40	25.0	5.4	29.2
Estimated Project Totals:		200		246.0	22.7	515.2

Mean = (a+ m +b) / 3   Variance = [(b - a) + (m - a) (m - b)] / 18

Beta Distribution (using PERT approximations)						
Initial Draft						
Gather Information	40	45	80	55.0	6.7	44.4
Write Sections	35	50	100	55.8	10.8	117.4
Review Informally	10	15	30	16.7	3.3	11.1
Inspection						
Inspectors Inspect	18	25	50	28.0	5.3	28.4
Prepare Defects/Issues List	10	20	40	21.7	5	25.0
Resolve Defects/Issues	10	25	60	28.3	8.3	69.4
Make Necessary Changes	15	20	40	22.5	4.2	17.4
Estimated Project Totals:		200		223.0	17.7	313.2

Mean = (a+ 4m +b) / 6   Variance = [(b - a) / 6]^2

When summing probability distributions:
 * If the distributions are skewed to the left as in this illustration, the project mean will always be significantly higher than the sum of the most likely estimates.
 * Distributions can be mixed and matched at will. The same distribution was used for all activities to simplify this illustration.

In order to sum probability distributions, calculate:
 * The mean, sigma (standard deviation), and variance for each individual activity based on the formula for that distribution (i.e., beta, triangular, flat, etc.).
 * The project mean as the sum of the individual activity means.
 * The project variance as the sum of the individual activity variances.
 * The project sigma (standard deviation) as the square root of the project variance.

In similar fashion, failure to include intangibles in this calculation can severely distort the result by equating a small loss with a high probability to a large loss with a small probability. The expected monetary value is generally used as input to further analysis (e.g., in a decision tree) since risk events can occur individually or in groups, in parallel or in sequence.

2- Statistical Sums

Statistical sums can be used to calculate a range of total project costs from the cost estimates for individual work items. (Calculating a range of probable project completion dates from the activity duration estimates requires simulation as described in Chapter 11). The range of total project costs can be used to quantify the relative risk of alternative project budgets or proposal prices. Figure 11-2 (Previous Page) illustrates the use of the "method of moments" technique to calculate project range estimates.

3- Simulation

Simulation uses a representation or model of a system to analyze the behavior or performance of the system. The most common form of simulation on a project is schedule simulation using the project network as the model of the project. Most schedule simulations are based on some form of Monte Carlo analysis. This technique, adapted from general management, "performs" the project many times to provide a statistical distribution of the calculated results as illustrated in Figure 11-3. The results of a schedule simulation may be used to quantify the risk of various schedule alternatives, different project strategies, different paths through the network, or individual activities.

Figure 11-3. Results from a Monte Carlo Simulation of a Project Schedule

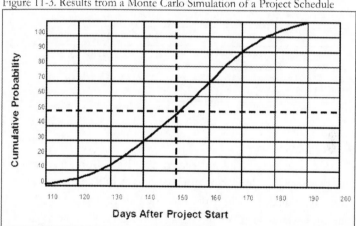

Schedule simulation should be used on any large or complex project since traditional mathematical analysis techniques such as the Critical Path Method (CPM) and the Program Evaluation and Review Technique (PERT) do not account for path convergence (see Figure 11-4) and thus tend to underestimate project durations. Monte Carlo analysis and other forms of simulation can also be used to assess the range of possible cost outcomes.

Figure 11-4. Path convergence

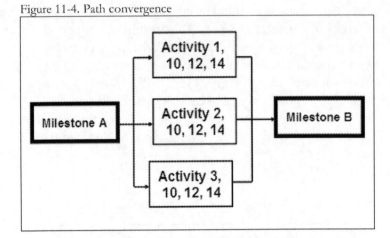

Activities 1,2 and 3 all have an expected duration of 12 days, ± 2 days. The CPM calculated duration of Milestone A to Milestone B is, therefore, 12 days. However, the actual duration will be greater than 12 days if any one of the activities is delayed. This is true even if the other activities finish in less than 12 days.

4- Decision Trees

A decision tree is a diagram that depicts key interactions among decisions and associated chance events as they are understood by the decision maker. The branches of the tree represent either decisions (shown as boxes) or chance events (shown as circles). Figure 11-5 is an example of a decision tree.

Figure 11-5. Decision Tree

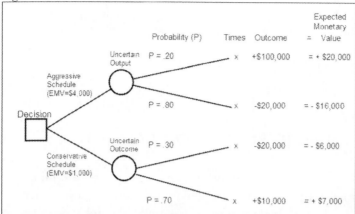

* Expected monetary value (EMV) of result = Outcome x Probability of that outcome.
* Expected monetary value of a decision = sum of EMVs of all Outcomes stemming from that decision
* Aggressive schedule has expected monetary value of $4,000 and is "perferred" over conservative schedule with expected monetary value of $1,000.

5- Expert Judgment

Expert judgment can often be applied in lieu of or in addition to the mathematical techniques described above. For example, risk events could be described as having a high, medium, or low probability of occurrence and a severe, moderate, or limited impact.

Results from Risk Quantification

1- Opportunities to Pursue, Threats to Respond to

The major output from risk quantification is a list of opportunities that should be pursued and threats that require attention.

2- Opportunities to Ignore, Threats to Accept

The risk quantification process should also document (a) those sources of risk and risk events that the project management team has consciously decided to accept or ignore and (b) who made the decision to do so.

RISK RESPONSE DEVELOPMENT

Risk response development involves defining enhancement steps for opportunities and responses to threats. Responses to threats generally fall into one of three categories:

- Avoidance - eliminating a specific threat, usually by eliminating the cause. The project management team can never eliminate all risk, but specific risk events can often be eliminated.
- Mitigation - reducing the expected monetary value of a risk event by reducing the probability of occurrence (e.g., using proven technology to lessen the probability that the product of the project will not work), reducing the risk event value (e.g., buying insurance), or both.
- Acceptance - accepting the consequences. Acceptance can be active (e.g., by developing a contingency plan to execute should the risk event occur) or passive (e.g., by accepting a lower profit if some activities overrun).

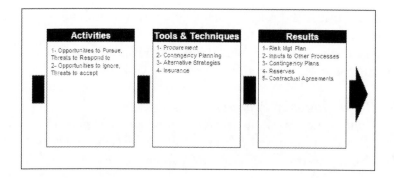

Activities to Risk Response Development

1- Opportunities to Pursue, Threats to Respond to
These are described in Chapter 11.

2- Opportunities to Ignore, Threats to Accept
These are described in Chapter 11. These items are input to the risk response development process because they should be documented in the risk management plan (described in Chapter 11).

Tools and Techniques for Risk Response Development

1- Procurement
Procurement, acquiring goods or services from outside the immediate project organization, is often an appropriate response to some types of risk. For example, risks associated with using a particular technology may be mitigated by contracting with an organization that has experience with that technology. Procurement often involves exchanging one risk for another. For example, mitigating cost risk with a fixed price contract may create

schedule risk if the seller is unable to perform. In similar fashion, trying to transfer all technical risk to the seller may result in an unacceptably high cost proposal. Project Procurement Management is described in Chapter 12.

2- Contingency Planning

Contingency planning involves defining action steps to be taken if an identified risk event should occur (see also the discussion of workarounds in Chapter 11).

3- Alternative Strategies

Risk events can often be prevented or avoided by changing the planned approach. For example, additional design work may decrease the number of changes which must be handled during the implementation or construction phase. Many application areas have a substantial body of literature on the potential value of various alternative strategies.

4- Insurance

Insurance or an insurance - like arrangement such as bonding is often available to deal with some categories of risk. The type of coverage available and the cost of coverage varies by application area.

Results from Risk Response Development

1- Risk Management Plan

The risk management plan should document the procedures that will be used to manage risk throughout the project. In addition to documenting the results of the risk identification and risk quantification processes, it should cover who is responsible for managing various areas of risk, how the initial identification and quantification outputs will be maintained, how contingency plans will be implemented, and how reserves will be allocated. A risk management plan may be formal or informal, highly detailed or broadly framed, based on the needs of the project. It is a subsidiary element of the overall project plan (described in Chapter 4).

2- Inputs to Other Processes

Selected or suggested alternative strategies, contingency plans, anticipated procurements, and other risk-related outputs must all be fed back into the appropriate processes in the other areas.

3- Contingency Plans

Contingency plans are pre-defined action steps to be taken if an identified risk event should occur. Contingency plans are generally part of the risk management plan, but they may also be integrated into other parts of the overall project plan (e.g., as part of a scope management plan or quality management plan).

4- Reserves

A reserve is a provision in the project plan to mitigate cost and/or schedule risk. The term is often used with a modifier (e.g., management reserve, contingency reserve, schedule reserve) to provide further detail on what types of risk are meant to be mitigated. The specific meaning of the modified terms often varies by application area. In addition, use of a reserve, and the definition of what may be included in a reserve, is also application-area-specific.

5- Contractual Agreements

Contractual agreements may be entered into for insurance, services, and other items as appropriate in order to avoid or mitigate threats. Contractual terms and conditions will have a significant effect on the degree of risk reduction.

RISK RESPONSE CONTROL

Risk response control involves executing the risk management plan in order to respond to risk events over the course of the project. When changes occur, the basic cycle of identify, quantify, and respond is repeated. It is important to understand that even the most thorough and comprehensive analysis cannot identify all risks and probabilities correctly; control and iteration are required.

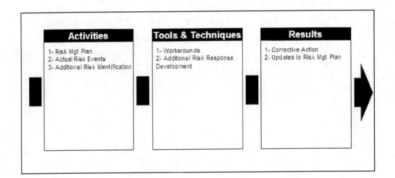

Activities to Risk Response Control

1- Risk Management Plan
The risk management plan is described in Chapter 11.

2- Actual Risk Events
Some of the identified risk events will occur, others will not. The ones that do are actual risk events or sources

of risk, and the project management team must recognize that one has occurred so that the response developed can be implemented.

3- Additional Risk Identification

As project performance is measured and reported (discussed in Chapter 10), potential risk events or sources of risk not previously identified may surface.

Tools and Techniques for Risk Response Control

1- Workarounds

Workarounds are unplanned responses to negative risk events. Workarounds are unplanned only in the sense that the response was not defined in advance of the risk event occurring.

2- Additional Risk Response Development

If the risk event was not anticipated, or the effect is greater than expected, the planned response may not be adequate, and it will be necessary to repeat the response development process and perhaps the risk quantification process as well.

Results from Risk Response Control

1- Corrective Action

Corrective action consists primarily of performing the planned risk response (e.g., implementing contingency plans or workarounds).

2- *Updates to Risk Management Plan*

As anticipated risk events occur or fail to occur, and as actual risk event effects are evaluated, estimates of probabilities and value, as well as other aspects of the risk management plan, should be updated.

CHAPTER 12

PROJECT PROCUREMENT MANAGEMENT

Project Procurement Management includes the processes required to acquire goods and services from outside the performing organization. For simplicity, goods and services, whether one or many, will generally be referred to as a "product." Figure 12-1 provides an overview of the following major processes:

- Procurement Planning - determining what to procure and when.
- Solicitation Planning - documenting product requirements and identifying potential sources.
- Solicitation - obtaining quotations, bids, offers, or proposals as appropriate.
- Source Selection - choosing from among potential sellers.
- Contract Administration - managing the relationship with the seller.
- Contract Close-out - completion and settlement of the contract, including resolution of any open items.

Figure 12-1. Project Procurement Management Overview

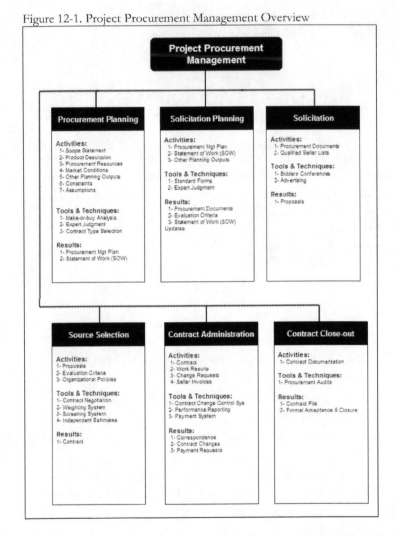

These processes interact with each other and with the processes in the other areas as well. Each process may involve effort from one or more individuals or groups of individuals based on the needs of the project. Although the processes are presented here as discrete elements with well-defined interfaces, in practice they may overlap and interact in ways not detailed here. Process interactions are discussed in detail in Chapter 3, Project Management Processes.

Project Procurement Management is discussed from the perspective of the buyer in the buyer-seller relationship. The buyer-seller relationship can exist at many levels on one project. Depending on the application area, the seller may be called a contractor, a vendor, or a supplier.

The *seller* will typically manage their work as a project. In such cases:

- The *buyer* becomes the customer and is thus a key stakeholder for the seller.
- The *seller's* project management team must be concerned with all the processes of project management, not just with those of this process area.
- The terms and conditions of the contract become a key input to many of the seller's processes. The contract may actually contain the input (e.g., major deliverables, key milestones, cost objectives) or it may limit the project team's options (e.g., buyer approval of staffing decisions is often required on design projects).

This chapter assumes that the seller is external to the performing organization. Most of the discussion, however, is equally applicable to *formal* agreements entered into with other units of the performing organization. When informal agreements are involved, the processes described in Project Human Resource Management, Chapter 9, and Project Communications Management, Chapter 10, are more likely to apply.

PROCUREMENT PLANNING

Procurement planning is the process of identifying which project needs can be best met by procuring products or services outside the project organization. It involves consideration of whether to procure, how to procure, what to procure, how much to procure, and when to procure it.

When the project obtains products and services from outside the performing organization, the processes from solicitation planning (Chapter 12) through contract close-out (Chapter 12) would be performed once for each product or service item. The project management team should seek support from specialists in the disciplines of contracting and procurement when needed. When the project does not obtain products and services from outside the performing organization, the processes from solicitation planning (Chapter 12) through contract close-out (Chapter 12) would *not* be performed. This often occurs on research and development projects when the performing organization is reluctant to share project technology and on many smaller, in-house projects when the cost of finding and managing an external resource may exceed the potential savings.

Procurement planning should also include consideration of potential subcontracts, particularly if the buyer wishes to exercise some degree of influence or control over subcontracting decisions.

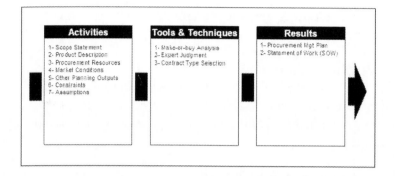

Activities to Procurement Planning

1- Scope Statement

The scope statement (see Chapter 5) describes the current project boundaries. It provides important information about project needs and strategies that must be considered during procurement planning.

2- Product Description

The description of the product of the project (described in Chapter 5) provides important information about any technical issues or concerns that would need to be considered during procurement planning. The product description is generally broader than a statement of work. A product description describes the ultimate end-product of the project; a statement of work (discussed in Chapter 12) describes the portion of that product to be provided by a seller to the project. However, if the performing organization chooses to procure the entire product, the distinction between the two terms becomes moot.

3- Procurement Resources

If the performing organization does not have a formal contracting group, the project team will have to supply both the, resources and the expertise to support project procurement activities.

4- Market Conditions

The procurement planning process must consider what products and services are available in the marketplace, from whom, and under what terms and conditions.

5- Other Planning Outputs

To the extent that other planning outputs are available, they must be considered during procurement planning. Other planning outputs which must often be considered include preliminary cost and schedule estimates, quality management plans, cash flow projections, the work breakdown structure, identified risks, and planned staffing.

6- Constraints

Constraints are factors that limit the buyer's options. One of the most common constraints for many projects is funds availability.

7- Assumptions

Assumptions are factors that, for planning purposes, will be considered to be true, real, or certain.

Tools and Techniques for Procurement Planning

1- Make-or-Buy Analysis

This is a general management technique which can be used to determine whether a particular product can be produced cost-effectively by the performing organization.

Both sides of the analysis include indirect as well as direct costs. For example, the "buy" side of the analysis should include both the actual out of pocket cost to purchase the product as well as the indirect costs of managing the purchasing process. A make-or-buy analysis must also reflect the perspective of the performing organization as well as the immediate needs of the project. For example, purchasing a capital item (anything from a construction crane to a personal computer) rather than renting it is seldom cost effective. However, if the performing organization has an ongoing need for the item, the portion of the purchase cost allocated to the project may be less than the cost of the rental.

2- Expert Judgment
Expert judgment will often be required to assess the inputs to this process. Such expertise may be provided by any group or individual with specialized knowledge or training and is available from many sources including:

- Other units within the performing organization.
- Consultants.
- Professional and technical associations.
- Industry groups.

3- Contract Type Selection
Different types of contracts are more or less appropriate for different types of purchases. Contracts generally fall into one of three broad categories:

- Fixed price or lump sum contracts - this category of contract involves a fixed total price for a well-defined product. To the extent that the product is not well-defined, both the buyer and seller are at risk-the buyer may not receive the desired product or the seller may need to incur additional costs in order to provide it. Fixed price contracts may also include incentives for meeting or exceeding selected project objectives such as schedule targets.

- Cost reimbursable contracts - this category of contract involves payment (reimbursement) to the seller for its actual costs. Costs are usually classified as *direct* costs or *indirect* costs. Direct costs are costs incurred for the exclusive benefit of the project (e.g., salaries of full-time project staff). Indirect costs, also called overhead costs, are costs allocated to the project by the performing organization as a cost of doing business (e.g.; salaries of corporate executives). Indirect costs are usually calculated as a percentage of direct costs. Cost reimbursable contracts often include incentives for meeting or exceeding selected project objectives such as schedule targets or total cost.

- Unit price contracts - the seller is paid a preset amount per unit of service (e.g., $70 per hour for professional services or $1.08 per cubic yard of earth removed), and the total value of the contract is a function of the quantities needed to complete the work.

Results from Procurement Planning

1- Procurement Management Plan

The procurement management plan should describe how the remaining procurement processes (from solicitation planning through contract close-out) will be managed. For example:

- What types of contracts will be used?
- If independent estimates will be needed as evaluation criteria, who will prepare them and when?
- If the performing organization has a procurement department, what actions can the project management team take on its own?
- If standardized procurement documents are needed, where can they be found?
- How will multiple providers be managed?
- How will procurement be coordinated with other project aspects such as scheduling and performance reporting?

A procurement management plan may be formal or informal, highly detailed or broadly framed, based on the needs of the project. It is a subsidiary element of the overall project plan described in Chapter 4, Project Plan Development.

2- Statement(s) of Work

The Statement of Work (SOW) describes the procurement item in sufficient detail to allow prospective sellers to determine if they are capable of providing the item. "Sufficient detail" may vary based on the nature of the item, the needs of the buyer, or the expected contract form. Some application areas recognize different types of SOW: For example, in some government jurisdictions, the term SOW is reserved for a procurement item that is a clearly specified product or service, and the term Statement of Requirements (SOR) is used for a procurement item that is presented as a problem to be solved.

The Statement of Work may be revised and refined as it moves through the procurement process. For example, a prospective seller may suggest a more efficient approach or a less costly product than that originally specified. Each individual procurement item requires a separate statement of work. However, multiple products or services may be grouped as one procurement item with a single SOW: The statement of work should be as clear, as complete, and as concise as possible.

It should include a description of any collateral services required, such as performance reporting or post-project operational support for the procured item. In some application areas, there are specific content and format requirements for a SOW:

SOLICITATION PLANNING

Solicitation planning involves preparing the documents needed to support solicitation (the solicitation process is described in Chapter 12).

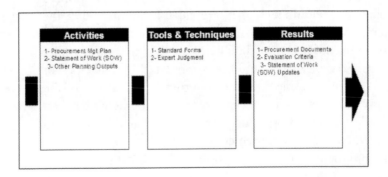

Activities to Solicitation Planning

1- Procurement Management Plan
The procurement management plan is described in Chapter 12.

2- Statement(s) of Work
The statement of work is described in Chapter 12.

3- Other Planning Outputs
Other planning outputs (see Chapter 12), which may have been modified from when they were considered as part of procurement planning, should be reviewed again as part of solicitation. In particular, solicitation planning should be closely coordinated with the project schedule.

Tools and Techniques for Solicitation Planning

1- Standard Forms
Standard forms may include standard contracts, standard descriptions of procurement items, or standardized versions of all or part of the needed bid documents (see Chapter 12). Organizations that do substantial amounts of procurement should have many of these documents standardized.

2- Expert Judgment
Expert judgment is described in Chapter 12.

Results from Solicitation Planning
1- Procurement Documents

Procurement documents are used to solicit proposals from prospective sellers. The terms "bid" and "quotation" are generally used when the source selection decision will be price-driven (as when buying commercial items), while the term "proposal" is generally used when non-financial considerations such as technical skills or approach are paramount (as when buying professional services).

However, the terms are often used interchangeably and care should be taken not to make unwarranted assumptions about the implications of the term used. Common names for different types of procurement documents include: Invitation for Bid (IFB), Request for Proposal (RFP), Request for Quotation (RFQ), Invitation for Negotiation, and Contractor Initial Response.

Procurement documents should be structured to facilitate accurate and complete responses from prospective sellers. They should always include the relevant statement of work, a description of the desired form of the response, and any required contractual provisions (e.g., a copy of a model contract, non-disclosure provisions). Some or all of the content and structure of procurement documents, particularly for those prepared by a government agency, may be defined by regulation.

Procurement documents should be rigorous enough to ensure consistent, comparable responses, but flexible enough to allow consideration of seller suggestions for better ways to satisfy the requirements.

2- Evaluation Criteria

Evaluation criteria are used to rate or score proposals. They may be objective (e.g., "the proposed project manager must be a certified Project Management Professional") or subjective (e.g., "the proposed project manager must have documented, previous experience with similar projects"). Evaluation criteria are often included as part of the procurement documents.

Evaluation criteria may be limited to purchase price if the procurement item is known to be readily available from a number of acceptable sources ("purchase price" in this context includes both the cost of the item and ancillary expenses such as delivery). When this is not the case, other criteria must be identified and documented to support an integrated assessment. For example:

- Understanding of need - as demonstrated by the seller's proposal.
- Overall or life cycle cost - will the selected seller produce the lowest total cost (purchase cost plus operating cost)?
- Technical capability - does the seller have, or can the seller be reasonably expected to acquire, the technical skills and knowledge needed?
- Management approach - does the seller have, or can the seller be reasonably expected to develop, management processes and procedures to ensure a successful project?
- Financial capacity - does the seller have, or can the seller reasonably be expected to obtain, the financial resources needed?

3- Statement of Work Updates

The statement of work is described in Chapter 12.

Modifications to one or more statements of work may be identified during solicitation planning.

SOLICITATION

Solicitation involves obtaining information (bids and proposals) from prospective sellers on how project needs can be met. Most of the actual effort in this process is expended by the prospective sellers, normally at no cost to the project.

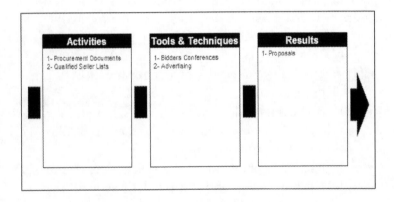

Activities to Solicitation

1- Procurement Documents
Procurement documents are described in Chapter 12.

2- Qualified Seller Lists
Some organizations maintain lists or files with information on prospective sellers. These lists will generally have information on relevant experience and

other characteristics of the prospective sellers. If such lists are not readily available, the project team will have to develop its own sources. General information is widely available through library directories, relevant local associations, trade catalogs, and similar sources. Detailed information on specific sources may require more extensive effort, such as site visits or contact with previous customers. Procurement documents may be sent to some or all of the prospective sellers.

Tools and Techniques for Solicitation

1- Bidder Conferences

Bidder conferences (also called contractor conferences, vendor conferences, and pre-bid conferences) are meetings with prospective sellers prior to preparation of a proposal. They are used to ensure that all prospective sellers have a clear, common understanding of the procurement (technical requirements, contract requirements, etc.). Responses to questions may be incorporated into the procurement documents as amendments.

2- Advertising

Existing lists of potential sellers can often be expanded by placing advertisements in general circulation publications such as newspapers or in specialty publications such as professional journals. Some government jurisdictions require public advertising of certain types of procurement items; most government jurisdictions require public advertising of subcontracts on a government contract.

Results from Solicitation

1- Proposals

Proposals (see also discussion of bids, quotations, and proposals in Chapter 12) are seller-prepared documents that describe the seller's ability and willingness to provide the requested product. They are prepared in accordance with the requirements of the relevant procurement documents.

SOURCE SELECTION

Source selection involves the receipt of bids or proposals and the application of the evaluation criteria to select a provider. This process is seldom straightforward:

- Price may be the primary determinant for an off-the-shelf item, but the lowest proposed *price* may not be the lowest *cost* if the seller proves unable to deliver the product in a timely manner.
- Proposals are often separated into technical (approach) and commercial (price) chapters with each evaluated separately.
- Multiple sources may be required for critical products.
- The tools and techniques described below may be used singly or in combination. For example, a weighting system may be used to:
- Select a single source who will be asked to sign a standard contract.
- Rank orders all proposals to establish a negotiating sequence.

On major procurement items, this process may be iterated. A short list of qualified sellers will be selected based on a preliminary proposal, and then a more detailed evaluation will be conducted based on a more detailed and comprehensive proposal.

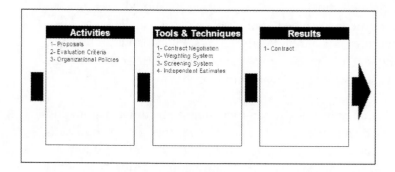

Activities to Source Selection

1- Proposals
Proposals are described in Chapter 12.

2- Evaluation Criteria
Evaluation criteria are described in Chapter 12.

3- Organizational Policies
Any and all of the organizations involved in the project may have formal or informal policies that can affect the evaluation of proposals.

Tools and Techniques for Source Selection

1- Contract Negotiation

Contract negotiation involves clarification and mutual agreement on the structure and requirements of the contract prior to the signing of the contract. To the extent possible, final contract language should reflect all agreements reached. Subjects covered generally include, but are not limited to, responsibilities and authorities, applicable terms and law, technical and business management approaches, contract financing, and price.

For complex procurement items, contract negotiation may be an independent process with inputs (e.g., an issues or open items list) and outputs (e.g., memorandum of understanding) of its own. Contract negotiation is a special case of the general management skill called "negotiation." Negotiation tools, techniques, and styles are widely discussed in the general management literature and are generally applicable to contract negotiation.

2- Weighting System

Weighting system is a method for quantifying qualitative data in order to minimize the effect of personal prejudice on source selection. Most such systems involve (1) assigning a numerical weight to each of the evaluation criteria, (2) rating the prospective sellers on each criterion, (3) multiplying the weight by the rating, and (4) totaling the resultant products to compute an overall score.

3- Screening System

A screening system involves establishing minimum requirements of performance for one or more of the evaluation criteria. For example, a prospective seller might be required to propose a project manager who is a Project

Management Professional (PMP) before the remainder of their proposal would be considered.

4- Independent Estimates

For many procurement items, the procuring organization may prepare its own estimates as a check on proposed pricing. Significant differences from these estimates may be an indication that the SOW was not adequate or that the prospective seller either misunderstood or failed to respond fully to the SOW Independent estimates are often referred to as "should cost" estimates.

Results from Source Selection

1- Contract

A contract is a mutually binding agreement which obligates the seller to provide the specified product and obligates the buyer to pay for it. *A contract is a legal relationship subject to remedy in the courts.* The agreement may be simple or complex, usually (bur not always) reflecting the simplicity or complexity of the product. It may be called, among other names, a contract, an agreement, a subcontract, a purchase order, or a memorandum of understanding. Most organizations have documented policies and procedures defining who can sign such agreements on behalf of the organization.

Although all project documents are subject to some form of review and approval, the legally binding nature of a contract usually means that it will be subjected to a more extensive approval process. In all cases, a primary focus of the review and approval process should be to ensure that the contract language describes a product or service that will satisfy the need identified. In the case of major projects undertaken by public agencies, the review process may even include public review of the agreement.

CONTRACT ADMINISTRATION

Contract administration is the process of ensuring that the seller's performance meets contractual requirements. On larger projects with multiple product and service providers, a key aspect of contract administration is managing the interfaces among the various providers. *The legal nature of the contractual relationship makes it imperative that the project team be acutely aware of the legal implications of actions taken when administering the contract.*

Contract administration includes application of the appropriate-project management processes to the contractual relationship(s) and integration of the outputs from these processes into the overall management of the project. This integration and coordination will often occur at multiple levels when there are multiple sellers and multiple products involved. The project management processes which must be applied include:

- Project plan execution, described in Chapter 4, to authorize the contractor's work at the appropriate time.
- Performance reporting, described in Chapter 10, to monitor contractor cost, schedule, and technical performance.
- Quality control, described in Chapter 8, to inspect and verify the adequacy of the contractor's product.

- Change control, described in Chapter 4, to ensure that changes are properly approved and that all those with a need to know are aware of such changes.

Contract administration also has a financial management component. Payment terms should be defined within the contract and should involve a specific linkage between progress made and compensation paid.

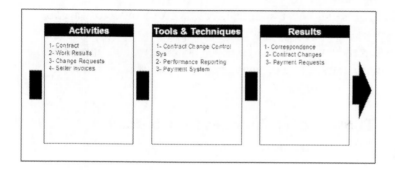

Activities to Contract Administration

1- Contract
Contracts are described in Chapter 12.

2- Work Results
The seller's work results - which deliverables have been completed and which have not, to what extent are quality standards being met, what costs have been incurred or committed, etc. - are collected as part of project plan execution (Chapter 4 provides more detail on project plan execution).

3- Change Requests

Change requests may include modifications to the terms of the contract or to the description of the product or service to be provided. If the seller's work is unsatisfactory, a decision to terminate the contract would also be handled as a change request. Contested changes, those where the seller and the project management team cannot agree on compensation for the change, are variously called claims, disputes, or appeals.

4- Seller Invoices

The seller must submit invoices from time to time to request payment for work performed. Invoicing requirements, including necessary supporting documentation, are usually defined in the contract.

Tools and Techniques for Contract Administration

1- Contract Change Control System

A contract change control system defines the process by which the contract may be modified. It includes the paperwork, tracking systems, dispute resolution procedures, and approval levels necessary for authorizing changes. The contract change control system should be integrated with the overall change control system (Chapter 4 describes the overall change control system).

2- Performance Reporting

Performance reporting provides management with information about how effectively the seller is achieving the contractual objectives. Contract performance reporting should be integrated with the overall project performance reporting described in Chapter 10.

3- Payment System

Payments to the seller are usually handled by the accounts payable system of the performing organization. On larger projects with many or complex procurement requirements, the project may develop its own system. In either case, the system must include appropriate reviews and approvals by the project management team.

Results from Contract Administration

1- Correspondence

Contract terms and conditions often require written documentation of certain aspects of buyer/seller communications, such as warnings of unsatisfactory performance and contract changes or clarifications.

2- Contract Changes

Changes (approved and unapproved) are fed back through the appropriate project planning and project procurement processes, and the project plan or other relevant documentation is updated as appropriate.

3- Payment Requests

This assumes that the project is using an external payment system. If the project has its own internal system, the output here would simply be "payments".

CONTRACT CLOSE-OUT

Contract close-out is similar to administrative closure (described in Chapter 10) in that it involves both product

verification (Was all work completed correctly and
satisfactorily?) and administrative close-out (updating of
records to reflect final results and archiving of such
information for future use). The contract terms and
conditions may prescribe specific procedures for contract
close-out. Early termination of a contract is a special case
of contract close-out.

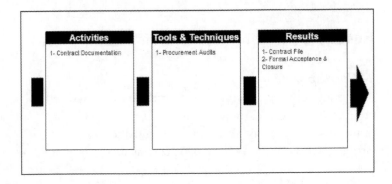

Activities to Contract Close-out

1- Contract Documentation
Contract documentation includes, but is not limited to,
    the contract itself along with all supporting schedules,
requested and approved contract changes, any seller-
developed technical documentation, seller performance
reports, financial documents such as invoices and payment
records, and the results of any contract-related inspections.

Tools and Techniques for Contract Close-out

1- Procurement Audits

A procurement audit is a structured review of the procurement process from procurement planning through contract administration. The objective of a procurement audit is to identify successes and failures that warrant transfer to other procurement items on this project or to other projects within the performing organization.

Results from Contract Close-out

2- Contract File

A complete set of indexed records should be prepared for inclusion with the final project records (see Chapter 10 for a more detailed discussion of administrative closure).

3- Formal Acceptance and Closure

The person or organization responsible for contract administration should provide the seller with formal written notice that the contract has been completed. Requirements for formal acceptance and closure are usually defined in the contract.

CHAPTER 13

APPLICATION DEVELOPMENT METHODOLOGY

A software development methodology refers to the framework that is used to structure, plan, and control the process of developing an information system. According to an online article titled Selecting a Development Approach (2008), "A wide variety of such frameworks have evolved over the years, each with its own recognized strengths and weaknesses. One system development methodology is not necessarily suitable for use by all projects. Each of the available methodologies is best suited to specific kinds of projects, based on various technical, organizational, project and team considerations". The framework of a software development methodology consists of:

- A software development philosophy, with the approach or approaches of the software development process.
- Multiple tools, models and methods, to assist in the software development process.

These frameworks are often bound to some kind of organization, which further develops, supports the use, and promotes the methodology. The methodology is often documented in some kind of formal documentation.

History

One of the oldest software development tools is flowcharting, which has its roots in the 1920s. The application software development methodology didn't emerge until the 1960s. According to Elliott (2004) the Systems Development Life Cycle (SDLC) can be considered to be the oldest formalized methodology for building information systems. The main idea of the SDLC has been "to pursue the development of information systems in a very deliberate, structured and methodical way, requiring each stage of the life cycle from inception of ideas to delivery of the final system, to be carried out in rigidly and sequentially". The main target of this methodology in the 1960s has been "to develop large scale functional business systems in an age of large scale business conglomerates. Information systems activities revolved around heavy data processing and number crunching routines".

Historical Dates for Software Development
In 1970s
- Structured programming since 1969

In 1980s
- Structured Systems Analysis and Design Methodology (SSADM) from 1980 onwards

In 1990s
- Object-Oriented Programming (OOP) has been developed since the early 1960s, and developed as the dominant programming methodology during the mid-1990s.
- Rapid Application Development (RAD) since 1991.
- Scrum (development), since the late 1990s

- Team software process developed by Watts Humphrey at the SEI.

In 2000s
  - Extreme Programming since 1999
  - Rational Unified Process (RUP) since 1998.
  - Agile Unified Process (AUP) since 2005 by Scott Ambler
  - Integrated Methodology (QAIassist-IM) since 2007
  - RAD used for more quickly software development.

Software development approaches

Every software development methodology has more or less its own approach to software development. There is a set of more general approaches, which are developed into several specific methodologies. These approaches are:

- **Waterfall**: linear framework type.
- **Prototyping**: iterative framework type
- **Incremental**: combination of linear and iterative framework type
- **Spiral**: combination linear and iterative framework type
- **Rapid Application Development (RAD)**: Iterative Framework Type

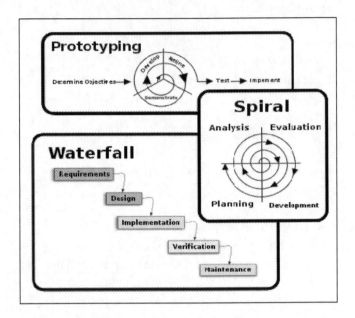

Waterfall Model

The waterfall model is a sequential development process, in which development is seen as flowing steadily downwards (like a waterfall) through the phases of requirements analysis, design, implementation, testing (validation), integration, and maintenance. The first formal description of the waterfall model is often cited to be an article published by Winston W. Royce (1987). Waterfall development is not new, it has been around since 1970, but most developers still only have a vague idea of what it means. Essentially, it's a framework for software development in which development proceeds sequentially through a series of phases, starting with system requirements analysis and leading up to product release and maintenance. Feedback loops exist between each phase, so that as new information is uncovered or problems are discovered, it is possible to "go back" a phase and make appropriate modification. Progress "flows" from one stage to the next, much like the waterfall that gives the model its name.

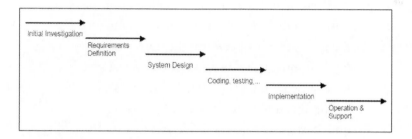

Basic principles:
- Project is divided into sequential phases, with some overlap and splash back acceptable between phases.
- Emphasis is on planning, time schedules, target dates, budgets and implementation of an entire system at one time.
- Tight control is maintained over the life of the project through the use of extensive written documentation, as well as through formal reviews and approval/signoff by the user and information technology management occurring at the end of most phases before beginning the next phase.

A number of variants of this model exist, with each one quoting slightly different labels for the various stages.

In general, however, the model may be considered as having six distinct phases, described below:

1. **Requirements analysis:** This first step is also the most important, because it involves gathering information about what the customer needs and defining, in the clearest possible terms, the problem that the product is expected to solve. Analysis includes understanding the customer's business context and constraints, the functions the product must perform, the performance levels it must adhere to, and the external systems it must be compatible with. Techniques used to obtain this understanding include customer interviews, use cases, and "shopping lists" of software features. The results of the analysis are typically captured in a formal requirements specification, which serves as input to the next step.

2. **Design:** This step consists of "defining the hardware and software architecture, components, modules, interfaces, and data to satisfy specified requirements" (Wikipedia). It involves defining the hardware and software architecture, specifying performance and security parameters, designing data storage containers and constraints, choosing the Integrated Development Environment (IDE) and programming language, and indicating strategies to deal with issues such as exception handling, resource management and

interface connectivity. This is also the stage at which user interface design is addressed, including issues relating to navigation and accessibility. The output of this stage is one or more design specifications, which are used in the next stage of implementation.

3. **Implementation:** This step consists of actually constructing the product as per the design specification(s) developed in the previous step. Typically, this step is performed by a development team consisting of programmers, interface designers and other specialists, using tools such as compilers, debuggers, interpreters and media editors. The output of this step is one or more product components, built according to a pre-defined coding standard and debugged, tested and integrated to satisfy the system architecture requirements. For projects involving a large team, version control is recommended to track changes to the code tree and revert to previous snapshots in case of problems.

4. **Testing:** In this stage, both individual components and the integrated whole are methodically verified to ensure that they are error-free and fully meet the requirements outlined in the first step. An independent quality assurance team defines "test cases" to evaluate whether the product fully or partially satisfies the requirements outlined in the first step. Three

types of testing typically take place;1) unit testing of individual code modules; 2) system testing of the integrated product; and 3) acceptance testing, formally conducted by or on behalf of the customer. Defects, if found, are logged and feedback provided to the implementation team to enable correction. This is also the stage at which product documentation, such as a user manual, is prepared, reviewed and published.

5. **Installation:** This step occurs once the product has been tested and certified as fit for use, and involves preparing the system or product for installation and use at the customer site. Delivery may take place via the Internet or physical media, and the deliverable is typically tagged with a formal revision number to facilitate updates at a later date.

6. **Maintenance:** This step occurs after installation, and involves making modifications to the system or an individual component to alter attributes or improve performance. These modifications arise either due to change requests initiated by the customer, or defects uncovered during live use of the system. Typically, every change made to the product during the maintenance cycle is recorded and a new product release (called a "maintenance release" and exhibiting an updated revision number) is performed to enable the customer to gain the benefit of the update.

Advantages

The waterfall model, according to Melonfire (2006), "offers numerous advantages for software developers". First, the staged development cycle enforces discipline; every phase has a defined start and end point, and progress can be conclusively identified (through the use of milestones) by both vendor and client. The emphasis on requirements and design before writing a single line of code ensures minimal wastage of time and effort and reduces the risk of schedule slippage, or of customer expectations not being met. Getting the requirements and design out of the way first also improves quality; it's much easier to catch and correct possible flaws at the design stage than at the testing stage, after all the components have been integrated and tracking down specific errors is more complex. Finally, because the first two phases end in the production of a formal specification, the waterfall model can aid efficient knowledge transfer when team members are dispersed in different locations. Other advantages of this model are:

1. Ideal for supporting less experienced project teams and project managers, or project teams whose composition fluctuates.
2. The orderly sequence of development steps and strict controls for ensuring the adequacy of documentation and design reviews helps ensure the quality, reliability, and maintainability of the developed software.
3. Progress of system development is measurable.
4. Conserves resources.

Disadvantages

Despite the seemingly obvious advantages, the waterfall model has come in for a fair share of criticism in recent times. The most prominent criticism revolves around the fact that very often, customers don't really know what they want up-front; rather, what they want emerges out of repeated two-way interactions over the course of the project. In this situation, the waterfall model, with its emphasis on up-front requirements capture and design, is seen as somewhat unrealistic and unsuitable for the vagaries of the real world. Further, given the uncertain nature of customer needs, estimating time and costs with any degree of accuracy (as the model suggests) is often extremely difficult. In general, therefore, the model is recommended for use only in projects which are relatively stable and where customer needs can be clearly identified at an early stage.

Another criticism revolves around the model's implicit assumption that designs can be feasibly translated into real products; this sometimes runs into roadblocks when developers actually begin implementation. Often, designs that look feasible on paper turn out to be expensive or difficult in practice, requiring a re-design and hence destroying the clear distinctions between phases of the traditional waterfall model.

Some criticisms also center on the fact that the waterfall model implies a clear division of labor between, say, "designers", "programmers" and "testers"; in reality, such a division of labor in most software firms is neither realistic nor efficient. Other disadvantages are as follow:

1. Inflexible, slow, costly and cumbersome due to significant structure and tight controls.
2. Project progresses forward, with only slight movement backward.
3. Little room for use of iteration, which can reduce manageability if used.
4. Depending upon early identification and specification of requirements, yet users may not be able to clearly define what they need early in the project.
5. Requirements inconsistencies, missing system components, and unexpected development needs are often discovered during design and coding.
6. Problems are often not discovered until system testing.
7. System performance cannot be tested until the system is almost fully coded, and under-capacity may be difficult to correct.
8. Difficult to respond to changes. Changes that occur later in the life cycle are more costly and are thus discouraged.
9. Produces excessive documentation and keeping it updated as the project progresses is time-consuming.
10. Written specifications are often difficult for users to read and thoroughly appreciate.
11. Promotes the gap between users and developers with clear division of responsibility.

Situations where most appropriate Using Waterfall Model:

1. Project is for development of a mainframe-based or transaction-oriented batch system.
2. Project is large, expensive, and complicated.
3. Project has clear objectives and solution.
4. Pressure does not exist for immediate implementation.
5. Project requirements can be stated unambiguously and comprehensively.
6. Project requirements are stable or unchanging during the system development life cycle.
7. User community is fully knowledgeable in the business and application.
8. Team members may be inexperienced.
9. Team composition is unstable and expected to fluctuate.
10. Project manager may not be fully experienced.
11. Resources need to be conserved.
12. Strict requirement exists for formal approvals at designated milestones.

Situations where least appropriate to Use Waterfall Model:

1. Large projects where the requirements are not well understood or are changing for any reasons such as external changes, changing expectations, budget changes or rapidly changing technology.
2. Web Information Systems (WIS) primarily due to the pressure of implementing a WIS project quickly; the continual evolution of the project requirements; the need for experienced, flexible team members drawn from multiple disciplines; and the inability to make assumptions regarding the users' knowledge level.

3. Real-time systems.
4. Event-driven systems.
5. Leading-edge applications.

Prototyping Model

Software prototyping is the framework of activities during software development of creating prototypes, i.e., incomplete versions of the software program being developed.

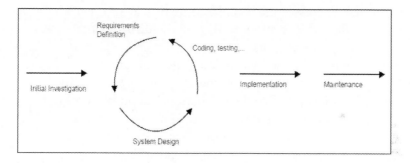

Basic principles:
- Not a standalone, complete development methodology, but rather an approach to handling selected portions of a larger, more traditional development methodology.
- Attempts to reduce inherent project risk by breaking a project into smaller segments and providing more ease-of-change during the development process.
- User is involved throughout the process, which increases the likelihood of user acceptance of the final implementation.
- Small-scale mock-ups of the system are developed following an iterative modification process until

the prototype evolves to meet the users'
requirements.

- While most prototypes are developed with the
  expectation that they will be discarded, it is
  possible in some cases to evolve from prototype to
  working system.
- A basic understanding of the fundamental business
  problem is necessary to avoid solving the wrong
  problem.

Advantages

1. "Addresses the inability of many users to specify
   their information needs, and the difficulty of
   systems analysts to understand the user's
   environment, by providing the user with a
   tentative system for experimental purposes at the
   earliest possible time." (Janson and Smith, 1985)
2. "Can be used to realistically model important
   aspects of a system during each phase of the
   traditional life cycle." (Huffaker, 1986)
3. Improves both user participation in system
   development and communication among project
   stakeholders.
4. Especially useful for resolving unclear objectives;
   developing and validating user requirements;
   experimenting with or comparing various design
   solutions; or investigating both performance and
   the human computer interface.
5. Potential exists for exploiting knowledge gained in
   an early iteration as later iterations are developed.
6. Helps to easily identify confusing or difficult
   functions and missing functionality.
7. May generate specifications for a production
   application.
8. Encourages innovation and flexible designs.

9. Provides quick implementation of an incomplete, but functional, application.

Disadvantages

1. Approval process and control is not strict.
2. Incomplete or inadequate problem analysis may occur whereby only the most obvious and superficial needs will be addressed, resulting in current inefficient practices being easily built into the new system.
3. Requirements may frequently change significantly.
4. Identification of non-functional elements is difficult to document.
5. Designers may prototype too quickly, without sufficient up-front user needs analysis, resulting in an inflexible design with narrow focus that limits future system potential.
6. Designers may neglect documentation, resulting in insufficient justification for the final product and inadequate records for the future.
7. Can lead to poorly designed systems. Unskilled designers may substitute prototyping for sound design, which can lead to a "quick and dirty system" without global consideration of the integration of all other components. While initial software development is often built to be a "throwaway", attempting to retroactively produce a solid system design can sometimes be problematic.
8. Can lead to false expectations, where the customer mistakenly believes that the system is "finished" when in fact it is not; the system looks good and has adequate user interfaces, but is not truly functional.

9. Iterations add to project budgets and schedules, thus the added costs must be weighed against the potential benefits. Very small projects may not be able to justify the added time and money, while only the high-risk portions of very large, complex projects may gain benefit from prototyping.
10. Prototype may not have sufficient checks and balances incorporated.

Situations where most appropriate to Use Prototyping Model

1. Project is for development of an online system requiring extensive user dialog, or for a less well-defined expert and decision support system.
2. Project is large with many users, interrelationships, and functions, where project risk relating to requirements definition needs to be reduced
3. Project objectives are unclear.
4. Pressure exists for immediate implementation of something.
5. Functional requirements may change frequently and significantly.
6. User is not fully knowledgeable.
7. Team members are experienced (particularly if the prototype is not a throw-away).
8. Team composition is stable.
9. Project manager is experienced.
10. No need exists to absolutely minimize resource consumption.
11. No strict requirement exists for approvals at designated milestones.
12. Analysts/users appreciate the business problems involved, before they begin the project.
13. Innovative, flexible designs that will accommodate future changes are not critical.

Situations where least appropriate to Use Prototyping Model

1. Mainframe-based or transaction-oriented batch systems.
2. Web-enabled e-business system.
3. Project team composition is unstable.
4. Future scalability of design is critic
5. Project objectives are very clear; project risk regarding requirements definition is low.

Incremental Model

Various methods are acceptable for combining linear and iterative systems development methodologies, with the primary objective of each being to reduce inherent project risk by breaking a project into smaller segments and providing more ease-of-change during the development process.

Basic principles of incremental development are:

- A series of mini-Waterfalls are performed, where all phases of the Waterfall development model are completed for a small part of the systems, before proceeding to the next incremental, or
- Overall requirements are defined before proceeding to evolutionary, mini-Waterfall development of individual increments of the system, or
- The initial software concept, requirements analysis, and design of architecture and system core are defined using the Waterfall approach, followed by iterative Prototyping, which culminates in installation of the final prototype (i.e., working system).

Advantages

1. Potential exists for exploiting knowledge gained in an early increment as later increments are developed.
2. Moderate control is maintained over the life of the project through the use of written documentation and the formal review and approval/signoff by the user and information technology management at designated major milestones.
3. Stakeholders can be given concrete evidence of project status throughout the life cycle.
4. Helps to mitigate integration and architectural risks earlier in the project.
5. Allows delivery of a series of implementations that are gradually more complete and can go into production more quickly as incremental releases.
6. Gradual implementation provides the ability to monitor the effect of incremental changes, isolate issues and make adjustments before the organization is negatively impacted.

Disadvantages

1. When utilizing a series of mini-Waterfalls for a small part of the system before moving on to the next increment, there is usually lack of overall consideration of the business problem and technical requirement s for the overall system.
2. Since some modules will be completed much earlier than others, well-defined interfaces are required.
3. Difficult problems tend to be pushed to the future to demonstrate early success to management.

Situations where most appropriate to Use Incremental Model

1. Large projects where requirements are not well understood or are changing due to external changes, changing expectations, budget changes or rapidly changing technology.
2. Web Information Systems (WIS) and event-driven systems.
3. Leading-edge applications.

Situations where least appropriate to Use Incremental Model

1. Very small projects of very short duration.
2. Integration and architectural risks are very low.
3. Highly interactive application where the data for the project already exists (completely or in part), and the project largely comprises analysis or reporting of the data.

Spiral Model

The spiral model is a software development process combining elements of both design and prototyping-in-stages, in an effort to combine advantages of top-down and

bottom-up concepts.

Basic principles:

• Focus is on risk assessment and on minimizing project risk by breaking a project into smaller segments and providing more ease-of-change during the development process, as well as providing the opportunity to evaluate risks and weigh consideration of project continuation throughout the life cycle.

- "Each cycle involves a progression through the same sequence of steps, for each portion of the product and for each of its levels of elaboration, from an overall concept-of-operation document down to the coding of each individual program." (Boehm, 1986).
- Each trip around the spiral traverses four basic quadrants: (1) determine objectives, alternatives, and constraints of the iteration; (2) Evaluate alternatives; Identify and resolve risks; (3) develop and verify deliverables from the iteration; and (4) plan the next iteration. (Boehm, 1986 and 1988).

- Begin each cycle with an identification of stakeholders and their win conditions, and end each cycle with review and commitment. (Boehm, 2000)

Advantages
1. Enhances risk avoidance.
2. Useful in helping to select the best methodology to follow for development of a given software iteration, based on project risk.

3. Can incorporate Waterfall, Prototyping, and Incremental methodologies as special cases in the framework, and provide guidance as to which combination of these models best fits a given software iteration, based upon the type of project risk. For example, a project with low risk of not meeting user requirements, but high risk of missing budget or schedule targets would essentially follow a linear Waterfall approach for a given software iteration. Conversely, if the risk factors were reversed, the Spiral methodology could yield an iterative Prototyping approach.

Disadvantages

1. Challenging to determine the exact composition of development methodologies to use for each iteration around the Spiral.
2. Highly customized to each project, and thus is quite complex, limiting reusability.
3. A skilled and experienced project manager is required to determine how to apply it to any given project.
4. There are no established controls for moving from one cycle to another cycle. Without controls, each cycle may generate more work for the next cycle.
5. There are no firm deadlines. Cycles continue with no clear termination condition, so there is an inherent risk of not meeting budget or schedule.
6. Possibility exists that project ends up implemented following a Waterfall framework.

Situations where most appropriate to Use Spiral Model

1. Real-time or safety-critical systems.
2. Risk avoidance is a high priority.

3. Minimizing resource consumption is not an
    absolute priority.
4. Project manager is highly skilled and experienced.
5. Requirement exists for strong approval and
    documentation control.
6. Project might benefit from a mix of other
    development methodologies.
7. A high degree of accuracy is essential.
8. Implementation has priority over functionality,
    which can be added in later versions.

Situations where least appropriate to Use Spiral Model

1. Risk avoidance is a low priority.
2. A high degree of accuracy is not essential.
3. Functionality has priority over implementation.
4. Minimizing resource consumption is an absolute
    priority.

Rapid Application Development (RAD) Model

Rapid Application Development (RAD) is a software
development methodology, which involves iterative
development and the construction of prototypes. Rapid
Application Development is a term originally used to
describe a software development process introduced by
James Martin in 1991.

Basic principles:
*   Key objective is for fast development and delivery
    of a high quality system at a relatively low
    investment cost.
*   Attempts to reduce inherent project risk by
    breaking a project into smaller segments and

providing more ease-of-change during the development process.

- Aims to produce high quality systems quickly, primarily through the use of iterative Prototyping (at any stage of development), active user involvement, and computerized development tools. These tools may include Graphical User Interface (GUI) builders, Computer Aided Software Engineering (CASE) tools, Database Management Systems (DBMS), fourth-generation programming languages, code generators, and object-oriented techniques.
- Key emphasis is on fulfilling the business need, while technological or engineering excellence is of lesser importance.
- Project control involves prioritizing development and defining delivery deadlines or "time boxes". If the project starts to slip, emphasis is on reducing requirements to fit the time box, not in increasing the deadline.
- Generally includes Joint Application Development (JAD), where users are intensely involved in system design, either through consensus building in structured workshops, or through electronically facilitated interaction.
- Active user involvement is imperative.
- Iteratively produces production software, as opposed to a throwaway prototype.
- Produces documentation necessary to facilitate future development and maintenance.
- Standard systems analysis and design techniques can be fitted into this framework.

Advantages

1. The operational version of an application is available much earlier than with Waterfall, Incremental, or Spiral frameworks.
2. Because RAD produces systems more quickly and to a business focus, this approach tends to produce systems at a lower cost.
3. Engenders a greater level of commitment from stakeholders, both business and technical, than Waterfall, Incremental, or Spiral frameworks. Users are seen as gaining more of a sense of ownership of a system, while developers are seen as gaining more satisfaction from producing successful systems quickly.
4. Concentrates on essential system elements from user viewpoint.
5. Provides the ability to rapidly change system design as demanded by users.
6. Produces a tighter fit between user requirements and system specifications
7. Generally produces a dramatic savings in time, money, and human effort.

Disadvantages

1. More speed and lower cost may lead to lower overall system quality.
2. Danger of misalignment of developed system with the business due to missing information.
3. Project may end up with more requirements than needed.
4. Potential for feature creep where more and more features are added to the system over the course of development.
5. Potential for inconsistent designs within and across systems.

6. Potential for violation of programming standards related to inconsistent naming conventions and inconsistent documentation.
7. Difficulty with module reuse for future systems.
8. Potential for designed system to lack scalability.
9. Potential for lack of attention to later system administration needs built into system.
10. High cost of commitment on the part of key user personnel.
11. Formal reviews and audits are more difficult to implement than for a complete system.
12. Tendency for difficult problems to be pushed to the future to demonstrate early success to management.
13. Since some modules will be completed much earlier than others, well-defined interfaces are required.

Situations where most appropriate to Use RAD Model

1. Project is of small-to-medium scale and of short duration (no more than 6 man-years of development effort).
2. Project scope is focused, such that the business objectives are well defined and narrow.
3. Application is highly interactive, has a clearly defined user group, and is not computationally complex.
4. Functionality of the system is clearly visible at the user interface.
5. Users possess detailed knowledge of the application area.
6. Senior management commitment exists to ensure end-user involvement.

7. Requirements of the system are unknown or uncertain.
8. It is not possible to define requirements accurately ahead of time because the situation is new or the system being employed is highly innovative.
9. Team members are skilled both socially and in terms of business.
10. Team composition is stable; continuity of core development team can be maintained.
11. Effective project control is definitely available.
12. Developers are skilled in the use of advanced tools.
13. Data for the project already exists (completely or in part), and the project largely comprises analysis or reporting of the data.
14. Technical architecture is clearly defined.
15. Key technical components are in place and tested.
16. Technical requirements (e.g., response times, throughput, database sizes, etc.) are reasonable and well within the capabilities of the technology being used. Targeted performance should be less than 70% of the published limits of the technology.
17. Development team is empowered to make design decisions on a day-to-day basis without the need for consultation with their superiors, and decisions can be made by a small number of people who are available and preferably co-located.

Situations where least appropriate to Use RAD Model

1. Very large, infrastructure projects; particularly large, distributed information systems such as corporate-wide databases.
2. Real-time or safety-critical systems.

3. Computationally complex systems, where complex and voluminous data must be analyzed, designed, and created within the scope of the project.
4. Project scope is broad and the business objectives are obscure.
5. Applications in which the functional requirements have to be fully specified before any programs are written.
6. Many people must be involved in the decisions on the project, and the decision makers are not available on a timely basis or they are geographically dispersed.
7. The project team is large or there are multiple teams whose work needs to be coordinated.
8. When user resource and/or commitment is lacking.
9. There is no project champion at the required level to make things happen.
10. Many new technologies are to be introduced within the scope of the project, or the technical architecture is unclear and much of the technology will be used for the first time within the project.
11. Technical requirements (e.g., response times, throughput, database sizes, etc.) are tight for the equipment that is to be used.

Other Software Development Approaches

Other method concepts are:

- Object oriented development methodologies, such as Grady Booch's Object-Oriented Design (OOD), also known as object-oriented analysis and design (OOAD). The Booch model includes stages such as: class, object, state transition, interaction, module, and process.

- Top-down programming: evolved in the 1970s by IBM researcher Harlan Mills (and Niklaus Wirth) in developed structured programming.
- Unified Process (UP) is an iterative software development methodology approach, based on UML. UP organizes the development of software into four phases, each consisting of one or more executable iterations of the software at that stage of development: Inception, Elaboration, Construction, and Guidelines. There are a number of tools and products available designed to facilitate UP implementation. One of the more popular versions of UP is the Rational Unified Process (RUP).

Business Processes

Graphical representation of the current state of information provides a very effective means for presenting information to both users and system developers.

Example of the interaction between business processes and data models.

- A business model illustrates the functions associated with the process being modeled and the organizations that perform these functions. By depicting activities and information flows, a foundation is created to visualize, define, understand, and validate the nature of a process.
- A data model provides the details of information to be stored, and is of primary use when the final product is the generation of computer software code for an application or the preparation of a functional specification to aid a computer software make-or-buy decision. See the figure "A" on the

right for an example of the interaction between business process and data models.

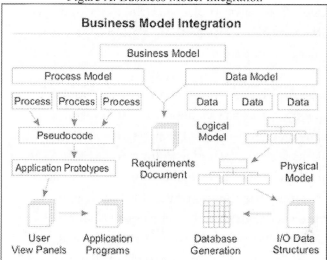

Figure A. Business Model Integration

Customer Needs

While each model does have advantages and disadvantages they all have certain degree of similarities for certain types of projects and can, when properly implemented, produce significant cost and time savings. Whether you should use it or not depends largely on how well you believe you understand your customer's needs, and how much volatility you expect in those needs as the project progresses.

Waterfall vs. RAD

The waterfall and Rapid Application Development (RAD) processes are most common methodologies that are available, but they generally predominate among methods used to deliver projects. Each has its individual merits, but sometimes one method is more appropriate for a particular project than the other.

Not all projects can be delivered with the waterfall methodology: plan, analyze, design, construct, and implement. In contrast, not all projects are candidates for RAD. Perhaps the best starting point is to take a look at some project characteristics that govern which method is best. One of the basic tenets of RAD is focusing on smaller projects that can be launched quickly and concluded with tangible deliveries. However, not all projects can be broken down into smaller pieces because they are too complex and interrelated to be split up effectively. There is no rule of thumb to determine how small a project needs to be before it is a candidate for RAD, but the larger you get; the harder it is to use the RAD model.

On the other extreme, if you have a small project to begin with, you might as well go quickly through the traditional waterfall process. If the requirements are not overly complex, document them all at once and be done with it, rather than go through a series of prototype steps to discover them all.

Who Needs a Prototype Model?

The beauty of the prototype model is that it provides an early look at the solution and it allows the customer to develop a better set of requirements through an iterative process. However, a prototype is not applicable with many projects. For instance, if your project involves implementing batch processes, there may not be much value to a prototype. Stick with the waterfall process on these projects. On the other hand, Web projects, because of their visual nature and the ability to reuse many components, lend themselves well to the RAD approach.

Packaged Solution Better?

The RAD methodology and the use of the prototype imply that you are building something. If you are implementing a packaged solution, a RAD approach probably will not work as well. It's also hard to break a package implementation into smaller pieces. In general, if you are working with a packaged solution, the waterfall approach is better. The exception is that the more customization that is done to a package, the more opportunity there is to use the package in a prototype mode and utilize RAD in general.

How Flexible is the Team?

The waterfall method is best when you want everything documented and you want to force all proposed changes through scope-change management. By its nature, RAD requires a high degree of flexibility and the ability to manage through change. For instance, your initial prototype may generate the type of discussion that will require the next version to be created completely from scratch. Organizations or teams that cannot adapt well to change should not use RAD.

Customer Participating in the Process?

The waterfall process requires heavy user involvement during planning, analysis, and testing. The RAD process requires the heavy involvement of customers in the phases of planning, analysis, and testing, and then over and over in the prototyping process. If you find it hard to engage the customers on an ongoing basis, then RAD and prototyping will not work for you.

Experienced Project Manager?

Although the project management processes may not be as rigorous, the cyclical nature of a RAD project requires a great deal of discipline and organization on the part of the project manager. If your project manager is inexperienced or does not possess strong organization skills, you probably do not want to undertake a RAD project. Stick to more traditional waterfall projects instead.

Selecting the Best Method

Most projects can be executed using the traditional waterfall process, and it is typically the safest approach. In fact, if it is appropriate, there are several techniques that can be used to accelerate project delivery with a waterfall approach. For instance, a large project can be split into smaller, more manageable pieces, with the subprojects utilizing waterfall methodology as well.

However, as described previously, many projects are candidates for RAD development. When there is a need for a good visual prototype, and when the users from business side engaged to define requirements quickly, it is possible to deliver a series of RAD projects sooner than one larger waterfall project. The customer also gets the added benefit of being able to use partial functionality very quickly as the earlier projects are delivered. During your planning process, examine the characteristics of each project to see if one development process will be more applicable than the other and then utilize the one best suited for your project.

REFERENCES

"A Survey of System Development Process Models";
Darryl Green and Ann DiCaterino; Center for Technology
in Government; February 1998;
(http://www.ctg.albany.edu/publications/reports/survey
of sysdev)

Crosby, Phillip B. *Quality is Free: The Art of Making Quality
Certain.* New York: McGraw-
Hill Book Company, 1979.

Crosby, Phillip B. *Quality is Still Free: Making Quality
Certain in Uncertain Times.* New
York: Mc-Graw-Hill Book Company, 1996.

Deming, W. Edwards. *Out of the Crisis.* Cambridge, MA:
Massachusetts Institute of
Technology Center for Advanced Engineering Study,
1986.

DeSimone, L.R. & Harris, M.D. Human resource
development. Pp. 32-33, 258-259. Orlando, FL.: Dryden
Press, 1998.

Duncan, William R. *A Guide To the Project Management Body
Of Knowledge.* Newtown Square, PA.: PMI Publishing,
1996.

Eccles, Robert, et al. *Beyond the Hype.* Cambridge, Mass.:
Harvard University Press, 1992

"Introduction to Systems Analysis, Topic 19, Rapid Application Development"; J. R. McBride; Copyright 2002 Prentice-Hall, Inc.;(http://www.csc.uvic.ca/~jmcbride/c375t19.pdf)

International Organization for Standardization (ISO). *Quality-Vocabulary (Draft International Standard 8402)*. Geneva, Switzerland: ISO Press, 1993.

International Organization for Standardization. *Code of Good Practice for Standardization (Draft International Standard)*. Geneva, Switzerland: ISO Press, 1994.

Iyigiin, M. Giiven. A Decision Support System' for R&D Project Selection and Resource Allocation Under Uncertainty. *Project Management Journal* (December), 1993.

Juran, Joseph M. *Juran on Planning for Quality*. New York: The Free Press, 1988.

Juran. Joseph M. *Juran on Quality by Design: The New Steps for Planning Quality into Goods and Services*. New York: The Free Press, 1992.

Kotter, John P. *A Force for Change: How Leadership Differs from Management*. New York, N.Y.: The Free Press, 1990.

Lynch, F.R. The diversity machine: the drive to change the white male workplace. New York. The Free Press, 1997.

Melonfire. *Project Management: Tools & Techniques, Development tools*, Software Development, 2006.

Mochal, Tom. *Waterfall vs. RAD: How to pick the right method for your project*. On-line, 2001.

Morris, Peter WG. Managing Project Interfaces: Key Points for Project Success. In Cleland and King, *Project Management Handbook,* Second Edition. Englewood Cliffs, N.: Prentice-Hall, 1981.

Muench, Dean. *The Sybase Development Framework.* Oakland, Calif.: Sybase Inc., 1994.

Murphy, Patrice L. Pharmaceutical Project Management: Is It Different? *Project Management Journal* (September), 1989.

Pfeffer, Jeffrey. *Managing with Power: Politics and Influence in Organizations.* HBS Press, 1992.

"Rapid Application Development: A Review and Case Study"; Paul Beynon-Davies; Kane Thompson Centre; December 1998; (http://www.comp.glam.ac.uk/SOC_Server/research/gis c/RADbrf1.htm)

Scope Definition and Control, Publication 6-2, p. 45. Austin, Tex.: Construction Industry Institute, 1986.

"System Development Life Cycle Models and Methodologies"; Paul Fisher, James McDaniel, and Peter Hughes; Canadian Society for International Health Certificate Course in Health Information Systems, Module 3: System Analysis & Database Development, Part 3: Life Cycle Models and Methodologies; (http://famed.ufrgs.br/pdf/csih/mod3/Mod_3_3.htm)

"System Development Methodologies for Web Enables E-Business: A Customization Paradigm"; Linda Night, Theresa Steinbach, and Vince Kellen: November 2001; (http://www.kellen.net/SysDev.htm)

Tan, D.L., Morris, L, & Romero, J. Changes in attitude after diversity training. Training & Development, 50(9). Pp. 54-55, 1996.

The American Heritage Dictionary of the English Language, Third Edition. Boston, Mass.: Houghton Mifflin Company, 1992.

Turner, Rodney. *The Handbook of Project-Based Management.* New York, N.Y.: McGraw-Hill, 1992.

Rovce, Winston W. W. *Managing the Development of Large Software Systems.* Edward Yourdon, 1987.

APPENDIX
A

Inclusions and Exclusions

This glossary includes terms that are:

- Unique or nearly unique to project management (e.g., scope statement, work package, work breakdown structure, critical path method).

- Not unique to project management, but used differently or with a narrower meaning in project management than in general everyday usage (e.g., early start date, activity, task).

This glossary generally does not include:

- Application area-specific terms (e.g., project prospectus as a legal document unique to real estate development).

- Terms whose use in project management does not differ in any material way from everyday use (e.g., contract).

- Compound terms whose meaning is clear from the combined meanings of the component parts.

- Variants when the meaning of the variant is clear from the base term (e.g., *exception report* is included, *exception reporting* is not).

As a result of the above inclusions and exclusions, this glossary includes:

- A preponderance of terms related to Project Scope Management and Project Time Management, since many of the terms used in these two knowledge areas are unique or nearly unique to project management.

- Many terms from Project Quality Management, since these terms are used more narrowly than in their everyday usage.

- Relatively few terms related to Project Human Resource Management, Project Risk Management, and Project Communications Management, since most of the terms used in these process areas do not differ significantly from everyday usage.

- Relatively few terms related to Project Cost Management and Project Procurement Management, since many of the terms used in these process areas have narrow meanings that are unique to a particular application area.

Common Acronyms

ACWP	- Actual Cost of Work Performed
AD	- Activity Description
ADM	- Arrow Diagramming Method
AF	- Actual Finish date
AOA	- Activity-On-Arrow
AON	- Activity-On-Node
AS	- Actual Start date
BAC	- Budget At Completion
BCWP	- Budgeted Cost of Work Performed
BCWS	- Budgeted Cost of Work Scheduled
CCB	- Change Control Board
CPFF	- Cost Plus Fixed Fee
CPIF	- Cost Plus Incentive Fee
CPI	- Cost Performance Index
CPM	- Critical Path Method
CV	- Cost Variance
DD	- Data Date
DU	- Duration
EAC	- Estimate At Completion
EF	- Early Finish date
ES	- Early Start date
ETC	- Estimate (or Estimated) To Complete (or Completion)
EV	- Earned Value
FF	- Free Float or Finish-to-Finish
FFP	- Firm Fixed Price
FPIF	- Fixed Price Incentive Fee
FS	- Finish-to-Start
GERT	- Graphical Evaluation and Review Technique
IFB	- Invitation For Bid
LF	- Late Finish date

LOE	- Level Of Effort
LS	- Late Start date
MPM	- Modern Project Management
OBS	- Organization(al) Breakdown Structure
PC	- Percent Complete
PDM	- Precedence Diagramming Method
PERT	- Program Evaluation and Review Technique
PF	- Planned Finish date
PM	- Project Management or Project Manager
PMP	- Project Management Professional
PS	- Planned Start date
QA	- Quality Assurance
QC	- Quality Control
RAM	- Responsibility Assignment Matrix
RD	- Remaining Duration
RFP	- Request For Proposal
RFQ	- Request For Quotation
SF	- Scheduled Finish date or Start-to-Finish
SOW	- Statement Of Work
SPI	- Schedule Performance Index
SS	- Scheduled Start date or Start-to-Start
SV	- Schedule Variance
TC	- Target Completion date
TF	- Total Float or Target Finish date
TS	- Target Start date
TQM	- Total Quality Management
WBS	- Work Breakdown Structure

APPENDIX
B

Terminology & Definitions

Many of the words defined here have broader, and in some cases different, dictionary definitions.
The definitions use the following conventions:

- Terms used as part of the definitions, and are defined in the glossary, are shown in *italics*.
- When synonyms are included, no definition is given and the reader is directed to the preferred term (i.e., see *preferred term*).
- Related terms that are not synonyms are cross-referenced at the end of the definition (i.e., see also *related term*).

Accountability Matrix. See *responsibility assignment matrix*.

Activity. An element of work performed during the course of a project. An activity normally has an expected duration, an expected cost, and expected resource requirements. Activities are often subdivided into tasks.

Activity Definition. Identifying the specific activities that must be performed in order to produce the various project deliverables.

Activity Description (AD). A short phrase or label used in a project network diagram. The activity description normally describes the scope of work of the activity.

Activity Duration Estimating. Estimating the number of work periods which will be needed to complete individual activities.

Activity-On-Arrow (AOA). See *arrow diagramming method.*

Activity-On-Node (AON). See *precedence diagramming method.*

Actual Cost of Work Performed (ACWP). Total costs incurred (direct and indirect) in accomplishing work during a given time period. See also *earned value.*

Actual Finish Date (AF). The point in time that work actually ended on an activity. (Note: in some application areas, the activity is considered "finished" when work is "substantially complete.")

Actual Start Date (AS). The point in time that work actually started on an activity.

Administrative Closure. Generating, gathering, and disseminating information to formalize project completion.

Application Area. A category of projects that have common elements not present in all projects. Application areas are usually defined in terms of either the product of the project (i.e., by similar technologies or industry sectors) or the type of customer (e.g., internal vs. external, government vs. commercial). Application areas often overlap.

Arrow. The graphic presentation of an activity. See also *arrow diagramming method.*

Arrow Diagramming Method (ADM). A network diagramming technique in which activities are represented by arrows. The tail of the arrow represents the start and the head represents the finish of the activity (the length of the arrow does *not* represent the expected duration of the activity). Activities are connected at points called nodes (usually drawn as small circles) to illustrate the sequence in which the activities are expected to be performed. See also *precedence diagramming method.*

As-of Date. See *data date.*

Backward Pass. The calculation of late finish dates and late start dates for the uncompleted portions of all network activities. Determined by working backwards through the network logic from the project's end date. The end date may be calculated in a *forward pass* or set by the customer or sponsor. See also *network analysis.*

Bar Chart. A graphic display of schedule-related information. In the typical bar chart, activities or other project elements are listed down the left side of the chart, dates are shown across the top, and activity durations are shown as date-placed horizontal bars. Also called a *Gantt chart.*

Baseline. The original plan (for a project, a work package, or an activity), plus or minus approved changes. Usually used with a modifier (e.g., cost baseline, schedule baseline, performance measurement baseline).

Baseline Finish Date. See *scheduled finish date.*

Baseline Start Date. See *scheduled start date.*

Budget At Completion (BAC). The estimated total cost of the project when done.

Budget Estimate. See *estimate.*

Budgeted Cost of Work Performed (BCWP). The sum of the approved cost estimates (including any overhead allocation) for activities (or portions of activities) completed during a given period (usually project-to-date). See also *earned value.*

Budgeted Cost of Work Scheduled (BCWS). The sum of the approved cost estimates (including any overhead allocation) for activities (or portions of activities) scheduled to be performed during a given period (usually project-to-date). See also *earned value.*

Calendar Unit. The smallest unit of time used in scheduling the project. Calendar units are generally in hours, days, or weeks, but can also be in shifts or even in minutes. Used primarily in relation to *project management software.*

Change Control Board (CCB). A formally constituted group of stakeholders responsible for approving or rejecting changes to the project *baselines.*

Change in Scope. See *scope change.*

Chart of Accounts. Any numbering system used to monitor project costs by category (e.g., labor, supplies, and materials). The project chart of accounts is usually based upon the corporate chart of accounts of the primary performing organization. See also *code of accounts.*
Charter. See *project charter.*

Code of Accounts. Any numbering system used to uniquely identify each element of the *work breakdown structure.* See also *chart of accounts.*

Communications Planning. Determining the information and communications needs of the project stakeholders.

Concurrent Engineering. An approach to project staffing that, in its most general form, calls for implementers to be involved in the design phase. Sometimes confused with *fast tracking.*

Contingencies. See *reserve* and *contingency planning.*

Contingency Allowance. See *reserve.*

Contingency Planning. The development of a management plan that identifies alternative strategies to be used to ensure project success if specified risk events occur.

Contingency Reserve. A separately planned quantity used to allow for future situations which may be planned for only in part (sometimes called "known unknowns"). For example, rework is certain, the amount of rework is not. Contingency reserves may involve cost, schedule, or both. Contingency reserves are intended to reduce the impact of missing cost or schedule objectives. Contingency reserves are normally included in the project's cost and schedule baselines.

Contract. A contract is a mutually binding agreement which obligates the seller to provide the specified product and obligates the buyer to pay for it. Contracts generally fall into one of three broad categories:

- Fixed price or lump sum contracts-this category of contract involves a fixed total price for a well-defined product. Fixed price contracts may also include incentives for meeting or exceeding selected project objectives such as schedule targets.
- Cost reimbursable contracts-this category of contract involves payment (reimbursement) to the contractor for its actual costs. Costs are usually classified as direct costs (costs incurred directly by the project, such as wages for members of the project team) and indirect costs (costs allocated to the project by the performing organization as a cost of doing business, such as salaries for corporate executives). Indirect costs are usually calculated as a percentage of direct costs. Cost reimbursable contracts often include incentives for meeting or exceeding selected project objectives such as schedule targets or total cost.
- Unit price contracts-the contractor is paid a preset amount per unit of service (e.g., $70 per hour for professional services or $1.08 per cubic yard of earth removed) and the total value of the contract is a function of the quantities needed to complete the work.

Contract Administration. Managing the relationship with the seller.

Contract Close-out. Completion and settlement of the contract, including resolution of all outstanding items.

Control. The process of comparing actual performance with planned performance, analyzing variances, evaluating possible alternatives, and taking appropriate *corrective action* as needed.

Control Charts. Control charts are a graphic display of the results, over time and against established control limits, of a process. They are used to determine if the process is "in control" or in need of adjustment.

Corrective Action. Changes made to bring expected future performance of the project into line with the plan.

Cost Budgeting. Allocating the cost estimates to individual project components.

Cost Control. Controlling changes to the project budget.

Cost Estimating. Estimating the cost of the resources needed to complete project activities.

Cost of Quality. The costs incurred to ensure quality. The cost of quality includes quality planning, quality control, quality assurance, and rework.

Cost Performance Index (CPI). The ratio of budgeted costs to actual costs (BCWP/ACWP).
CPI is often used to predict the magnitude of a possible cost overrun using the following formula: original cost estimate/CPI = projected cost at completion. See also *earned value.*

Cost Plus Fixed Fee (CPFF) Contract. A type of *contract* where the buyer reimburses the seller for the seller's allowable costs (allowable costs are defined by the contract) plus a fixed amount of profit (fee).

Cost Plus Incentive Fee (CPIF) Contract. A type of *contract* where the buyer reimburses the seller for the seller's allowable costs (allowable costs are defined by the contract), and the seller earns its profit if it meets defined performance criteria.

Cost Variance (CV). (1) Any difference between the estimated cost of an activity and the actual cost of that activity. (2) In *earned value*, BCWP less ACWP.

Crashing. Taking action to decrease the total project duration after analyzing a number of alternatives to determine how to get the maximum duration compression for the least cost.

Critical Activity. Any activity on a *critical path*. Most commonly determined by using the *critical path method*. Although some activities are "critical" in the dictionary sense without being on the critical path, this meaning is seldom used in the project context.

Critical Path. In a *project network diagram*, the series of activities which determines the earliest completion of the project. The critical path will generally change from time to time as activities are completed ahead of or behind schedule. Although normally calculated for the entire project, the critical path can also be determined for a *milestone* or *subproject*. The critical path is usually defined as those activities with float less than or equal to a specified value, often zero. See *critical path method*.

Critical Path Method (CPM). A *network analysis* technique used to predict project duration by analyzing which sequence of activities (which *path)* has the least amount of scheduling flexibility (the least amount of *float)*. Early dates are calculated by means of a *forward pass* using a specified start date. Late dates are calculated by means of a *backward pass* starting from a specified completion date (usually the forward pass's calculated project *early finish date*).

Current Finish Date. The current estimate of the point in time when an activity will be completed.

Current Start Date. The current estimate of the point in time when an activity will begin.

Data Date (DO). The point in time that separates actual (historical) data from future (scheduled) data. Also called *as-of date*.

Definitive Estimate. See *estimate*.

Deliverable. Any measurable, tangible, verifiable outcome, result, or item that must be produced to complete a project or part of a project. Often used more narrowly in reference to an *external deliverable*, which is a deliverable that is subject to approval by the project sponsor or customer.

Dependency. See *logical relationship*.

Dummy Activity. An activity of zero duration used to show a *logical relationship* in the *arrow diagramming method*. Dummy activities are used when logical relationships cannot be completely or correctly described with regular activity arrows. Dummies are shown graphically as a dashed line headed by an arrow.

Duration (DU). The number of work periods (not including holidays or other non-working periods) required to complete an activity or other project element. Usually expressed as workdays or workweeks. Sometimes incorrectly equated with elapsed time. See also *effort*.

Duration Compression. Shortening the project schedule without reducing the project scope.
Duration compression is not always possible and often requires an increase in project cost.

Early Finish Date (EF). In the *critical path method*, the earliest possible point in time on which the uncompleted portions of an activity (or the project) can finish based on the network logic and any schedule constraints. Early finish dates can change as the project progresses and changes are made to the project plan.

Early Start Date (ES). In the *critical path method*, the earliest possible point in time on which the uncompleted portions of an activity (or the project) can start, based on the network logic and any schedule constraints. Early start dates can change as the project progresses and changes are made to the project plan.

Earned Value (EV). (1) A method for measuring project performance. It compares the amount of work that was planned with what was actually accomplished to determine if cost and schedule performance is as planned. See also *actual cost of work performed, budgeted cost of work scheduled, budgeted cost of work performed, cost variance, cost performance index, schedule variance,* and *schedule performance index.* (2) The *budgeted cost of work performed* for an activity or group of activities.

Earned Value Analysis. See definition (1) under *earned value.*

Effort. The number of labor units required to complete an activity or other project element. Usually expressed as staff-hours, staff-days, or staff-weeks. Should not be confused with *duration*.

Estimate. An assessment of the likely quantitative result. Usually applied to project costs and durations and should always include some indication of accuracy (e.g., $\pm$ x percent). Usually used with a modifier (e.g., preliminary, conceptual, feasibility). Some application areas have specific modifiers that imply particular accuracy ranges (e.g., order-of-magnitude estimate, budget estimate, and definitive estimate in engineering and construction projects).

Estimate At Completion (EAC). The expected total cost of an activity, a group of activities, or of the project when the defined scope of work has been completed. Most techniques for forecasting EAC include some adjustment of the original cost estimate based on project performance to date. Also shown as "estimated at completion." Often shown as EAC = Accruals-to-date + ETC. See also *earned value* and *estimate to complete*.

Estimate To Complete (ETC). The expected additional cost needed to complete an activity, a group of activities, or the project. Most techniques for forecasting ETC include some adjustment to the original estimate based on project performance to date. Also called "estimated to complete." See also *earned value* and *estimate at completion*.

Event-on-Node. A network diagramming technique in which events are represented by boxes (or nodes) connected by arrows to show the sequence in which the events are to occur. Used in the original *Program Evaluation and Review Technique*.

Exception Report. Document that includes only major variations from plan (rather than all variations).

Expected Monetary Value. The product of an event's probability of occurrence and the gain or loss that will result. For example, if there is a 50 percent probability that it will rain, and rain will result in a $100 loss, the expected monetary value of the rain event is $50 (.5 x $100).

Fast Tracking. Compressing the project schedule by overlapping activities that would normally be done in sequence, such as design and construction. Sometimes confused with *concurrent engineering*.

Finish Date. A point in time associated with an activity's completion. Usually qualified by one of the following: actual, planned, estimated, scheduled, early, late, baseline, target or current.

Finish-to-Finish (FF). See *logical relationship*.

Finish-to-Start (FS). See *logical relationship*.

Firm Fixed Price (FFP) Contract. A type of *contract* where the buyer pays the seller a set amount (as defined by the contract) regardless of the seller's costs.

Fixed Price Contract. See *firm fixed price contract*.

Fixed Price Incentive Fee (FPIF) Contract. A type of *contract* where the buyer pays the seller a set amount (as defined by the contract), and the seller can earn an additional amount if it meets defined performance criteria.

Float. The amount of time that an activity may be delayed from its early start without delaying the project finish date. Float is a mathematical calculation and can change as the project progresses and changes are made to the project plan. Also called slack, total float, and path float. See also *free float*.

Forecast Final Cost. See *estimate at completion*.

Forward Pass. The calculation of the early start and early finish dates for the uncompleted portions of all network activities. See also *network analysis* and *backward pass*.

Fragnet. See *subnet*.

Free Float (FF). The amount of time an activity can be delayed without delaying the *early start* of any immediately following activities. See also *float*.

Functional Manager. A manager responsible for activities in a specialized department or function (e.g., engineering, manufacturing, marketing).

Functional Organization. An organization structure in which staff are grouped hierarchically by specialty (e.g., production, marketing, engineering, and accounting at the top level; with engineering, further divided into mechanical, electrical, and others).

Gantt Chart. See *bar chart*.

Grade. A category or rank used to distinguish items that have the same functional use (e.g., "hammer") but do not share the same requirements for quality (e.g., different hammers may need to withstand different amounts of force).

Graphical Evaluation and Review Technique (GERT). A *network analysis* technique that allows for conditional and probabilistic treatment of *logical relationships* (i.e., some activities may not be performed).

Hammock. An aggregate or summary activity (a group of related activities is shown as one and reported at a summary level). A hammock mayor may not have an internal sequence. See also *subproject* and *subnet*.

Hanger. An unintended break in a *network path*. Hangers are usually caused by missing *activities* or missing *logical relationships*.

Information Distribution. Making needed information available to project stakeholders in a timely manner.

Initiation. Committing the organization to begin a project phase.

Integrated Cost/Schedule Reporting. See *earned value*.

Invitation for Bid (IFB). Generally, this term is equivalent to *request for proposal*. However, in some application areas it may have a narrower or more specific meaning.

Key Event Schedule. See *master schedule*.

Lag. A modification of a *logical relationship* which directs a delay in the successor task. For example,
in a finish-to-start dependency with a 10-day lag, the successor activity cannot start until 10 days after the predecessor has finished. See also *lead*.

Late Finish Date (LF). In the *critical path method*, the latest possible point in time that an activity may be completed without delaying a specified milestone (usually the project finish date).

Late Start Date (LS). In the *critical path method*, the latest possible point in time that an activity may begin without delaying a specified milestone (usually the project finish date).

Lead. A modification of a *logical relationship* which allows an acceleration of the successor task. For example, in a finish-to-start dependency with a 10-day lead, the successor activity can start 10 days before the predecessor has finished. See also *lag*.

Level of Effort (LOE). Support-type activity (e.g., vendor or customer liaison) that does not readily lend itself to measurement of discrete accomplishment. It is generally characterized by a uniform rate of activity over a specific period of time.

Leveling. See *resource leveling*.

Life-cycle Costing. The concept of including acquisition, operating, and disposal costs when evaluating various alternatives.

Line Manager. (1) The manager of any group that actually makes a product or performs a service.
(2) A *functional manager*.

Link. See *logical relationship*.

Logic. See *network logic*.

Logic Diagram. See *project network diagram*.

Logical Relationship. A dependency between two project activities, or between a project activity and a milestone. See also *precedence relationship*. The four possible types of logical relationships are:

- Finish-to-start-the "from" activity must finish before the "to" activity can start.
- Finish-to-finish-the "from" activity must finish before the "to" activity can finish.
- Start-to-start-the "from" activity must start before the "to" activity can start.
- Start-to-finish-the "from" activity must start before the "to" activity can finish.

Loop. A *network path* that passes the same node twice. Loops cannot be analyzed using traditional *network analysis* techniques such as *CPM* and *PERT*. Loops are allowed in *GERT*.

Management Reserve. A separately planned quantity used to allow for future situations which are impossible to predict (sometimes called "unknown unknowns"). Management reserves may involve cost or schedule. Management reserves are intended to reduce the risk of missing cost or schedule objectives. Use of management reserve requires a change to the project's cost baseline.

Master Schedule. A *summary-level schedule* which identifies the major activities and key milestones. See also *milestone schedule*.

Mathematical Analysis. See *network analysis*.

Matrix Organization. Any organizational structure in which the project manager shares responsibility with the functional managers for assigning priorities and for directing the work of individuals assigned to the project.

Milestone. A significant event in the project, usually completion of a major deliverable.

Milestone Schedule. A summary-level schedule which identifies the major milestones. See also *master schedule.*

Mitigation. Taking steps to lessen risk by lowering the probability of a risk event's occurrence or reducing its effect should it occur.

Modern Project Management (MPM). A term used to distinguish the current broad range of project management (scope, cost, time, quality, risk, etc.) from narrower, traditional use that focused on cost and time.

Monitoring. The capture, analysis, and reporting of project performance, usually as compared to plan.

Monte Carlo Analysis. A schedule risk assessment technique that performs a project simulation many times in order to calculate a distribution of likely results.

Near-Critical Activity. An *activity* that has low total *float.*
Network. See *project network diagram.*

Network Analysis. The process of identifying early and late start and finish dates for the uncompleted portions of project activities. See also *Critical Path Method, Program Evaluation and Review Technique,* and *Graphical Evaluation and Review Technique.*

Network Logic. The collection of activity dependencies that make up a *project network diagram.*

Network Path. Any continuous series of connected activities in a *project network diagram.*

Node. One of the defining points of a network; a junction point joined to some or all of the other dependency lines. See also *arrow diagramming method* and *precedence diagramming method.*

Order of Magnitude Estimate. See *estimate.*

Organizational Breakdown Structure (OBS). A depiction of the project organization arranged so as to relate *work packages* to organizational units.

Organizational Planning. Identifying, documenting, and assigning project roles, responsibilities, and reporting relationships.

Overall Change Control. Coordinating changes across the entire project.

Overlap. See *lead.*

Parametric Estimating. An estimating technique that uses a statistical relationship between historical data and other variables (e.g., square footage in construction, lines of code in software development) to calculate an estimate.

Pareto Diagram. A histogram, ordered by frequency of occurrence, that shows how many results were generated by each identified cause.

Path. A set of sequentially connected activities in a *project network diagram.*

Path Convergence. In mathematical analysis, the tendency of parallel paths of approximately equal duration to delay the completion of the milestone where they meet.

Path Float. See *float.*

Percent Complete (PC). An estimate, expressed as a percent, of the amount of work which has been completed on an activity or group of activities.

Performance Reporting. Collecting and disseminating information about project performance to help ensure project progress.

Performing Organization. The enterprise whose employees are most directly involved in doing the work of the project.

PERT Chart. A specific type of *project network diagram.* See *Program Evaluation and Review Technique.*

Phase. See *project phase.*

Planned Finish Date (PF). See *scheduled finish date.*

Planned Start Date (PS). See *scheduled start date.*

Precedence Diagramming Method (PDM). A network diagramming technique in which activities are represented by boxes (or nodes). Activities are linked by *precedence relationships* to show the sequence in which the activities are to be performed.

Precedence Relationship. The term used in the *precedence diagramming method* for a *logical relationship*. In current usage, however, precedence relationship, logical relationship, and dependency are widely used interchangeably regardless of the diagramming method in use.

Predecessor Activity. (1) In the *arrow diagramming method*, the activity which enters a *node*. (2) In the *precedence diagramming method*, the "from" activity.

Procurement Planning. Determining what to procure and when.

Program. A group of related projects managed in a coordinated way. Programs usually include an element of ongoing activity.

Program Evaluation and Review Technique (PERT). An event-oriented *network analysis* technique used to estimate project duration when there is a high degree of uncertainty with the individual activity duration estimates. PERT applies the *critical path method* to a weighted average duration estimate. Also given as *Program Evaluation and Review Technique.*

Project. A temporary endeavor undertaken to create a unique product or service.

Project Charter. A document issued by senior management that provides the project manager with the authority to apply organizational resources to project activities.

Project Communications Management. A subset of project management that includes the processes required to ensure proper collection and dissemination of project information. It consists of *communications planning, information distribution, performance reporting,* and *administrative closure.*

Project Cost Management. A subset of project management that includes the processes required to ensure that the project is completed within the approved budget. It consists of *resource planning, cost estimating, cost budgeting,* and *cost control.*

Project Human Resource Management. A subset of project management that includes the processes required to make the most effective use of the people involved with the project. It consists of *organizational planning, staff acquisition,* and *team development.*

Project Integration Management. A subset of project management that includes the processes required to ensure that the various elements of the project are properly coordinated. It consists of *project plan development, project plan execution,* and *overall change control.*

Project Life Cycle. A collection of generally sequential *project phases* whose name and number are determined by the control needs of the organization or organizations involved in the project.

Project Management (PM). The application of knowledge, skills, tools, and techniques to project activities in order to meet or exceed stakeholder needs and expectations from a project.

Project Management Body of Knowledge. An inclusive term that describes the sum of knowledge within the profession of project management. As with other professions such as law, medicine, and accounting, the body of knowledge rests with the practitioners and academics who apply and advance it. The project management includes proven, traditional practices which are widely applied as well as innovative and advanced ones which have seen more limited use.

Project Management Professional (PMP). An individual certified as such by the Project Management Institute.

Project Management Software. A class of computer applications specifically designed to aid with planning and controlling project costs and schedules.

Project Management Team. The members of the project team who are directly involved in project management activities. On some smaller projects, the project management team may include virtually all of the *project team members.*

Project Manager (PM). The individual responsible for managing a project.

Project Network Diagram. Any schematic display of the logical relationships of project activities. Always drawn from left to right to reflect project chronology. Often incorrectly referred to as a "PERT chart."

Project Phase. A collection of logically related project activities, usually culminating in the completion of a major *deliverable.*

Project Plan. A formal, approved document used to guide both project execution and project control. The primary uses of the project plan are to document planning assumptions and decisions, to facilitate communication among stakeholders, and to document approved scope, cost, and schedule baselines. A project plan may be summary or detailed.

Project Plan Development. Taking the results of other planning processes and putting them into a consistent, coherent document.

Project Plan Execution. Carrying out the project plan by performing the activities included therein.

Project Planning. The development and maintenance of the *project plan.*

Project Procurement Management. A subset of project management that includes the processes required to acquire goods and services from outside the performing organization. It consists of *procurement planning, solicitation planning, solicitation, source selection, contract administration,* and *contract close-out.*

Project Quality Management. A subset of project management that includes the processes required to ensure that the project will satisfy the needs for which it was undertaken. It consists of *quality planning, quality assurance,* and *quality control.*

Project Risk Management. A subset of project management that includes the processes concerned with identifying, analyzing, and responding to project risk. It consists of *risk identification, risk quantification, risk response development,* and *risk response control.*

Project Schedule. The planned dates for performing activities and the planned dates for meeting milestones.

Project Scope Management. A subset of project management that includes the processes required to ensure that the project includes all of the work required, and only the work required, to complete the project successfully. It consists of *initiation, scope planning, scope definition, scope verification,* and *scope change control.*

Project Team Members. The people who report either directly or indirectly to the project manager.

Project Time Management. A subset of project management that includes the processes required to ensure timely completion of the project. It consists of *activity definition, activity sequencing, activity duration estimating, schedule development,* and *schedule control.*

Project-based Organization. Any organizational structure in which the project manager has full authority to assign priorities and to direct the work of individuals assigned to the project.

Quality Assurance (QA). (1) The process of evaluating overall project performance on a regular basis to provide confidence that the project will satisfy the relevant quality standards. (2) The organizational unit that is assigned responsibility for quality assurance.

Quality Control (QC). (1) The process of monitoring specific project results to determine if they comply with relevant quality standards and identifying ways to eliminate causes of unsatisfactory performance. (2) The organizational unit that is assigned responsibility for quality control.

Quality Planning. Identifying which quality standards are relevant to the project and determining how to satisfy them.

Remaining Duration (RDU). The time needed to complete an activity.

Request for Proposal (RFP). A type of bid document used to solicit proposals from prospective sellers of products or services. In some application areas it may have a narrower or more specific meaning.

Request for Quotation (RFQ). Generally, this term is equivalent to *request for proposal.* However, in some application areas it may have a narrower or more specific meaning.

Reserve. A provision in the project plan to mitigate cost and/or schedule risk. Often used with a modifier (e.g., *management reserve, contingency reserve)* to provide further detail on what types of risk are meant to be mitigated. The specific meaning of the modified term varies by *application area.*

Resource Leveling. Any form of *network analysis* in which scheduling decisions (start and finish dates) are driven by resource management concerns (e.g., limited resource availability or difficult-to-manage changes in resource levels).

Resource-Limited Schedule. A project schedule whose start and finish dates reflect expected resource availability. The final project schedule should always be resource-limited.

Resource Planning. Determining what resources (people, equipment, materials) are needed in what quantities to perform project activities.

Responsibility Assignment Matrix (RAM). A structure which relates the project organization structure to the *work breakdown structure* to help ensure that each element of the project's scope of work is assigned to a responsible individual.

Responsibility Chart. See *responsibility assignment matrix.*

Responsibility Matrix. See *responsibility assignment matrix.*

Retainage. A portion of a contract payment that is held until contract completion in order to ensure full performance of the contract terms.

Risk Event. A discrete occurrence that may affect the project for better or worse.

Risk Identification. Determining which risk events are likely to affect the project.

Risk Quantification. Evaluating the probability of risk event occurrence and effect.

Risk Response Control. Responding to changes in risk over the course of the project.

Risk Response Development. Defining enhancement steps for opportunities and mitigation steps for threats.

S-Curve. Graphic display of cumulative costs, labor hours, or other quantities, plotted against time. The name derives from the S-like shape of the curve (flatter at the beginning and end, steeper in the middle) produced on a project that starts slowly, accelerates, and then tails off.

Schedule. See *project schedule.*

Schedule Analysis. See *network analysis.*

Schedule Compression. See *duration compression.*

Schedule Control. Controlling changes to the project schedule.

Schedule Development. Analyzing activity sequences, activity durations, and resource requirements to create the project schedule.

Schedule Performance Index (SPI). The ratio of work performed to work scheduled (BCWP/BCWS). See *earned value.*

Schedule Variance (SV). (1) Any difference between the scheduled completion of an activity and the actual completion of that activity. (2) In *earned value,* BCWP less BCWS.

Scheduled Finish Date (SF). The point in time work was scheduled to finish on an activity. The scheduled finish date is normally within the range of dates delimited by the *early finish date* and the *late finish date.*

Scheduled Start Date (SS). The point in time work was scheduled to start on an activity. The scheduled start date is normally within the range of dates delimited by the *early start date* and the *late start date.*

Scope. The sum of the products and services to be provided as a project.

Scope Baseline. See *baseline.*

Scope Change. Any change to the project scope. A scope change almost always requires an adjustment to the project cost or schedule.

Scope Change Control. Controlling changes to project scope.

Scope Definition. Decomposing the major deliverables into smaller, more manageable components to provide better control.

Scope Planning. Developing a written scope statement that includes the project justification, the major deliverables, and the project objectives.

Scope Verification. Ensuring that all identified project deliverables have been completed satisfactorily.

Should-Cost Estimates. An *estimate* of the cost of a product or service used to provide an assessment of the reasonableness of a prospective contractor's proposed cost.

Slack. Term used in *PERT* for *float.*

Solicitation. Obtaining quotations, bids, offers, or proposals as appropriate.

Solicitation Planning. Documenting product requirements and identifying potential sources.

Source Selection. Choosing from among potential contractors.

Staff Acquisition. Getting the human resources needed assigned to and working on the project.

Stakeholder. Individuals and organizations who are involved in or may be affected by project activities.

Start Date. A point in time associated with an activity's start, usually qualified by one of the following: actual, planned, estimated, scheduled, early, late, target, baseline, or current.

Start-to-Finish. See *logical relationship*.

Start-to-Start. See *logical relationship*.

Statement of Work (SOW). A narrative description of products or services to be supplied under contract.
Subnet. A subdivision of a *project network diagram* usually representing some form of subproject.

Sub-network. See *subnet*.

Successor Activity. (1) In the *arrow diagramming method*, the activity which departs a node. (2) In the *precedence diagramming method*, the "to" activity.

Target Completion Date (TC). An imposed date which constrains or otherwise modifies the *network analysis*.

Target Schedule. See *baseline*.

Task. See *activity*.

Team Development. Developing individual and group skills to enhance project performance.

Team Members. See *project team members*.

Time-Scaled Network Diagram. Any *project network diagram* drawn in such a way that the positioning and length of the activity represents its duration. Essentially, it is a bar chart that includes *network logic*.

Target Finish Date (TF). The date work is planned (targeted) to finish on an activity.

Target Start Date (TS). The date work is planned (targeted) to start on an activity.

Total Float (TF). See *float*.

Total Quality Management (TOM). A common approach to implementing a quality improvement program within an organization.

Workaround. A response to a negative risk event. Distinguished from *contingency plan* in that a workaround is not planned in advance of the occurrence of the risk event.

Work Breakdown Structure (WBS). A deliverable-oriented grouping of project elements which organizes and defines the total scope of the project. Each descending level represents an increasingly detailed definition of a project component. Project components may be products or services.

Work Item. See *activity*.

Work Package. A deliverable at the lowest level of the *work breakdown structure*. A work package may be divided into activities.

APPENDIX
C

SUMMARY
OF BASIS FOR PROJECT MANAGEMENT

Project Integration Management

A subset of project management that includes the processes required to ensure that the various elements of the project are properly coordinated. It consists of:

- Project Plan Development: Taking the results of other planning processes and putting them into a consistent, coherent document.
- Project Plan Execution: Carrying out the project plan by performing the activities included therein.
- Overall Change Control: Coordinating changes across the entire project.

Project Scope Management

A subset of project management that includes the processes required to ensure that the project includes all the work required, and to complete the project successfully. It consists of:

- Scope Planning: Developing a written scope statement as the basis for future project decisions.
- Scope Definition: Subdividing the major project deliverables into smaller, more manageable components.
- Scope Verification: Formalizing acceptance of the project scope.
- Scope Change Control: Controlling changes to project scope.

Project Time Management

A subset of project management that includes the processes required to ensure timely completion of the project. It consists of:

- Activity Definition: Identifying the specific activities that must be performed to produce the various project deliverables.

- Activity Sequencing: Identifying and documenting interactivity dependencies.

- Activity Duration Estimating: Estimating the number of work periods which will be needed to complete individual activities.

- Schedule Development: Analyzing activity sequences, activity durations, and resource requirements to create the project schedule.

- Schedule Control: Controlling changes to the project schedule.

Project Cost Management

A subset of project management that includes the processes required to ensure that the project is completed within the approved budget. It consists of:

- Resource Planning: Determining what resources (people, equipment, materials) and what quantities of each should be used to perform project activities.

- Cost Estimating: Developing an approximation (estimate) of the costs of the resources needed to complete project activities.

- Cost Budgeting: Allocating the overall cost estimate to individual work items.

- Cost Control: Controlling changes to the project budget.

Project Quality Management

A subset of project management that includes the processes required to ensure that the project will satisfy the needs for which it was undertaken. It consists of:

- Quality Planning: Identifying which quality standards are relevant to the project and determining how to satisfy them.
- Quality Assurance: Evaluating overall project performance on a regular basis to provide confidence that the project will satisfy the relevant quality standards.
- Quality Control: Monitoring specific project results to determine if they comply with relevant quality standards and identifying ways to eliminate causes of unsatisfactory performance.

Project Human Resource Management

A subset of project management that includes the processes required to make the most effective use of the people involved with the project. It consists of:

- Organizational Planning: Identifying, documenting, and assigning project roles, responsibilities, and reporting relationships.
- Staff Acquisition: Getting the human resources needed assigned to and working on the project.
- Team Development: Developing individual and group skills to enhance project performance.

Project Communications Management

A subset of project management that includes the processes required to ensure timely and appropriate generation, collection, dissemination, storage, and ultimate disposition of project information. It consists of:

- Communications Planning: Determining the information and communications needs of the stakeholders who needs what information, when will they need it, and how will it be given to them.
- Information Distribution: Making needed information available to project stakeholders in a timely manner.
- Performance Reporting: Collecting and disseminating performance information. This includes status reporting, progress measurement, and forecasting.
- Administrative Closure: Generating, gathering, and disseminating information to formalize phase or project completion.

Project Risk Management

A subset of project management that includes the processes concerned with identifying, analyzing, and responding to project risk. It consists of:

- Risk Identification: Determining which risks are likely to affect the project and documenting the characteristics of each.
- Risk Quantification: Evaluating risks and risk interactions to assess the range of possible project outcomes.
- Risk Response Development: Defining enhancement steps for opportunities and responses to threats.

- Risk Response Control: Responding to changes in risk over the course of the project.

Project Procurement Management

A subset of project management that includes the processes required to acquire goods and services from outside the performing organization. It consists of:

- Procurement Planning: Determining what to procure and when.
- Solicitation Planning: Documenting product requirements and identifying potential sources.
- Solicitation: obtaining quotations, bids, offers, or proposals as appropriate.
- Source Selection: Choosing from among potential sellers.
- Contract Administration: Managing the relationship with the seller.
- Contract Close-out: Completion and settlement of the contract, including resolution of any open items.

Application Development Methodologies

- Waterfall: Linear framework type.
- Prototyping: Iterative framework type
- Incremental: Combination of linear and iterative framework type
- Spiral: Combination linear and iterative framework type
- Rapid Application Development (RAD): Iterative framework type